AF447865

RAISING AN ADDICT

A Memoir

FAITH ADDAIR

Published by Isaiah 26:3 Publishing

Cover Artwork: Luke Sassani
Cover Design: Robin Axtell
Editing and Interior Design: Michele Chynoweth

ISBN: 979-8-218-37845-5

CONTENTS

DEDICATION

To my beautiful momma,
I wish I had let you read what I wrote before you left us,
but you can see it all now and I know that you are proud.
Thank you for loving me and believing in me.
I miss you so much, but I will see you again one day,
because like you, "I'm going to heaven."

ACKNOWLEDGMENTS

This book has taken more years than I care to admit to finally get out and into the hands of the public. I would like to thank God, who gave me this idea and then would not let me start anything else until I finished it. Without Him, this story would be very different.

To my husband, Kenny, who has always been by my side, cheering me on, holding me up, loving me and encouraging me, you are my best friend and the love of my life. God truly blessed me the day He sent you to me. I love you so much!

To our son, we are so proud of you and grateful for your dedication to staying clean. You are a great son and a terrific dad and husband. We love you so much.

To our daughter, I will be forever grateful for you and your love and support during this time in our lives. Dad and I love you.

To my friends and family who encouraged and nagged me to hurry up and get this done, I heard you and I hope I didn't mess it up!

To Pastor Phil Meekins, who helped us in too many ways to try and list. You are dearly missed.

Thank you, Luke Sassani, for allowing me to use your artwork for the cover.

And finally, I'd like to thank my book coach, editor, and friend, Michele Chynoweth. Thank you for never giving up on me. Your knowledge and encouragement are priceless. I know this book would have taken much longer without you.

CHAPTER ONE

LOOKING INTO HIS EYES

"It's a boy! It's a boy!" my husband, Kenny, cheered excitedly. He was right. On that beautiful spring day in 1994, I looked into the sweet eyes of our newborn son. A son that we really began to give up hope of ever having. After Kenny and I had suffered the heartbreaks of losing four babies through miscarriages, God had finally blessed us with a healthy baby girl almost two years earlier. But when I had another miscarriage about six months after she was born, I lost faith in ever giving birth again.

But here he was, perfect and red and angry to be out in this cold world. His cries could be heard over the din of all the nurses and students in our room at Harford Memorial Hospital.

Dr. Swanbeck smiled at Kenny and I, his yellow paper gown hanging off his shoulder, his hat askew and barely staying on his head. "This one was in a hurry, but he made it! Congratulations guys."

The doctor's eyes glistened with genuine happiness. He knew how much this baby meant to our family because he had helped us through several of our losses.

Our family was complete. I looked down at our squalling baby and then gazed up at Kenny who was smiling down at me, his tired but joyful gray eyes shining with tears. I had only seen tears in my husband's eyes one other time and that was when our beautiful daughter Autumn came into this world. This strong husband of mine looked at me like I had performed some kind of miracle, and maybe I did.

"Look at how strong he looks!" Kenny said. "His little shoulders and chest are so broad."

As we looked at Kadin's little ruddy-colored body, the dreams of what he would become one day were flying through my head. I know Kenny was already imagining him swinging a sledgehammer and putting up tents for the party rental company he and his buddy Eric were planning to start in the next few years. I knew my husband hoped this son of ours would grow up and start working alongside him, dad and son.

Me? I believe from the beginning I was thinking, I just don't want him to get hurt, I just want to protect him.

Even as a little kid, Kadin's eyes were always the mirror to what was going on inside. I could look at him and tell if he was getting sick, if he was mad or sad or telling a fib. Those big, innocent chocolate brown eyes also were able to turn me into mush and make me want to give him whatever he wanted. This was evident when, as kids, his older sister, Autumn, wanted something—she would usually send Kadin to ask. I don't know if they ever realized that I was onto that ploy. But Lord knows it worked more than a few times through the years.

Kadin was so excited to start Pre-K as he watched his sister get on the bus every day. "When do I get to go on the yellow school bus, Mama?" he'd ask me daily.

As I would help him pick up the many Hot Wheels cars he would bring to the bus stop at the end of the driveway, I'd look down into those little pleading brown eyes and tell him, "Soon baby, soon." But my heart cried silently, don't grow up too soon, just wait a little longer please. I even had the bright idea of getting him a little book bag to put all his cars in to carry to the bus stop so he could feel like one of the "big" kids.

Watching him actually get on the school bus that first day, though, was bittersweet—my baby was finally getting to go to school. When the bus pulled up to our driveway that morning, for a brief moment I watched Kadin's little brown eyes filled with fear.

Autumn was coaxing her little brother as she climbed the steps into the bus ahead of him. "Come on Kadin, it's no big deal." Then she was gone, headed back to her seat as he watched.

"Go ahead." I nodded to him and smiled, touching his shoulder to guide him to the bus. "I love you baby. You are going to have so much fun!"

"Love you Mommy," he said quietly, looking resigned to head towards what must have seemed to him like no less than a firing squad.

He looked back at me only once and gave me a little grimacing smile, but his eyes were so uncertain. As he started to climb up the steps of the bus, his little legs strained to reach that first one. He looked so small, so helpless, but he made it and with one last little wave at me disappeared to go find his seat.

Dear Lord, help him…help me…get through this day. I walked back to the house sobbing like an idiot.

As I stood on the front porch waiting for the bus to pass back by, I thought, if I see that he still looks sad, I'll just wave down the bus and go get him off and we will try again tomorrow. I could hear the bus coming back up the road and as it rumbled along, I strained to see my kids through the small windows. I saw Autumn waving, her little sweet round face smiling at me...and then saw Kadin, his back turned to me, apparently talking to someone, not even looking my way.

"That little stinker!" I muttered out loud. Here I am worried sick for the longest five minutes of my life and he's playing with the kid behind him and has already forgotten about me. What the heck? But I went back into the house relieved that he was okay.

Not long after the school year began, his Pre-Kindergarten teacher contacted us. "Kadin likes to talk and unfortunately he is disrupting the classroom," she said over the phone. "He is a smart little guy for a four-year-old. He can tell me his ABCs and count well, but when he has to write anything down on paper it is a challenge for him. So, his grades are starting to suffer." She sighed into the phone. I could hear her frustration. We worked with him every night after that. One night I was helping him with his letters, but he just wasn't understanding me and what I was asking him to do. His little face looked so sad because he knew I was frustrated with him.

"Kadin, you have to pay attention and try harder!" I said sharply.

"I'm trying Mommy." He glanced up at me, his sweet little round face silently pleading for help.

"You have to try harder." I tried unsuccessfully to keep the exasperation I felt, out of my voice.

He looked back down at the paper that he was working on, and a tear plopped onto it.

I had to leave the kitchen table where we were working and find my husband Kenny.

"Oh my God," I growled to my big teddy bear of a guy. "I can't get him to do his work. He knows the answers when I ask him, but he doesn't want to write it down, then when he does it's so sloppy I have to erase it and make him do it over."

"Okay, he's only four, Faith." Kenny responded calmly, hugging me.

"I know that." I could feel my anger rise. "But he has to get this done and done right!" I snapped, pushing him away. "Now he's crying and making me feel like an ogre. I need you to go help him for a while before I lose it." I walked away from my husband in a huff. Why do I have to handle everything? I am always the bad guy.

I heard them working together at the kitchen table, as I folded laundry in the adjoining living room of our double wide trailer. The light outside was dimming as night drew closer. Kenny and Kadin continued to work on the homework assignment as I walked past them into the kitchen to start making dinner.

"Just take your time buddy and make sure that you are writing as neatly as you can, okay?" Kenny leaned back in the dining room chair, looked at me and smiled.

They were talking calmly, and even joking around and laughing, and I felt a stab of jealousy prick my heart. What is wrong with me? I'm his mother. I felt like I had failed Kadin. I had nearly screamed out loud in my impatience. What's the difference between him and Autumn? I wondered as I pounded the ground beef that would soon be meatloaf. I could usually help my daughter and not get too frustrated. But I just couldn't help my son.

As I finished getting dinner ready, I marveled at Kadin as he put away his homework and skipped through the family room as if he didn't have a problem in the world. He was happy that his homework was done and it was dinner time, until he found out it was meatloaf night.

"How'd you do buddy?" I asked him as I put dinner on the table.

"Good, I'm all done." He looked at what I had put on the table and his smile fell. "Oh man, meatloaf? Yuck!"

Throughout dinner I noticed that Kenny was quiet. He didn't look up from his plate other than to say, "Good dinner hon," and then his eyes immediately fell back down.

Later that night, Kenny walked into our bedroom and sighed heavily. I was sitting up propped against the pillows, trying to read a new Nora Roberts novel, but had just read the same paragraph for the fourth time.

"I think we need to have Kadin's eyes checked." Kenny sat wearily on the edge of the bed in his jeans and plaid flannel shirt, his big shoulders slumped over.

"Why do you think that?" I asked him defensively, tossing my book onto the bed. After all, I'm his mother. I would know that before anyone else.

"He's having a very hard time seeing, Faith. He was squinting at the paper. His face kept getting closer to it as I was showing him things and asking questions."

"I know but he's so young." I got up off the bed and walked around to his side and looked at him. At five-foot-four compared to his six-foot stature, I was almost eye level with Kenny as he sat on the bed and looked at me.

"I recognize the signs, Faith." My gentle giant answered as he adjusted his own glasses on his face.

I faltered for a moment. "How do they even test a kid this young? He doesn't even know all the alphabet yet!" I started getting more agitated.

"I don't know but if they can test babies, they can test him." He muttered sadly as he got up and walked into the master bathroom.

As we left the eye doctor at the Walmart in Abingdon, Maryland a little over a week later, the doctor's questions were still racing through my head.

"Does he stumble and fall a lot?" he asked.

"Well yes, but he is a little boy who never stops moving." I chuckled weakly.

The doctor didn't skip a beat. "Does he stand or sit really close to the TV?"

"Yes, he does," I said in a most serious tone. "But we always tell him to back up because sitting that close will make his eyes go bad."

"That's not really true nowadays, but it is usually a good sign there is already a sight issue." He jotted down a note in his manilla file folder. "Does he hold books or pictures close to his face or get close to your face when he is talking to you?"

I hesitated, the light of truth beginning to dawn in my defensive brain. "Yes, he does." Oh my gosh, how could I have missed all those signs? Was I blind? Was I even paying attention to my baby?

The kind doctor must have seen my distress and shame and tried to reassure me that these signs were all quite easy to miss at this age and I thanked him for that. But I knew in my heart I had failed Kadin.

He explained how bad Kadin's eyes were and that my son would probably have to wear glasses or contacts for the rest of his life.

Two weeks later we picked up Kadin's new pair of glasses. I knew from the conversation with the doctor that his eyesight was quite bad…but I didn't realize how much he wasn't seeing until I put them on his sweet, chubby little face and it lit up, those big brown eyes literally bugged out of it. His little head looked like it was on a swivel going back and forth looking from one thing to another. The smile on his face said it all— Hello world!

As I lifted him into our old red and white 1972 Ford Bronco to go home, he put his little hands on either side of my face and squeezed just a little. As he looked at me. he exclaimed with surprise and concern, "Mommy, you have holes in your head!" and his tiny fingers gently touched the twenty-two-year-old chicken pox scars on my forehead between my eyes.

"Yes baby," I choked out, barely holding onto the sob that caught in my throat. I stroked his sandy brown hair, tucking it behind his little ears. I cupped his round cheeks and looked up at him. His normally olive toned skin was golden brown from the sun. "That's from chicken pox when I was a little girl about your age. Remember when you and Autumn had them and your Mitsy stuffed dog got them too?" I had put red spots on his favorite stuffed animal. "Remember me telling you not to scratch and pick at them?"

"Yeah, I think so," he answered, already distracted.

"Well, this is why I didn't want you to scratch or pick at them, so you wouldn't have scars like this from it."

"Oh." I fastened his seat belt, watching him look with fascination out of his car window.

When I got in and put my seat belt on, it took a few minutes for me to collect myself. Tears fell and I shook with quiet sobs all the way home.

How did I not know that my precious baby couldn't see?

How was it that today was the first day that our four-year-old child could actually see me clearly? Wonder and guilt turned to full-blown anger at myself.

How horrible am I that my child couldn't see for so long? How did I miss the signs? What kind of mother am I?

Little did I know this wouldn't be the last time I would ask myself these questions.

The following Monday, Kadin got on the school bus and as I watched the bus full of kids pass by, my little boy was standing up and looking around as if it was the first time he was really seeing everything—because it was.

We expected that at his age, we would be replacing glasses every other month, but we were wrong. Kadin loved his glasses because they helped him see. He wore those glasses everywhere—even to bed and into the shower.

"You have to be very careful with your glasses, so they don't get broken, okay?" Kenny and I explained to him.

"I know." And he really was very careful with them because he knew he needed them to be able to see clearly.

I wonder today if he thinks, I have to be careful not to put myself in a position to lose my sobriety because I need to see clearly…

CHAPTER TWO

SEEING THE SIGNS

"Our brains are like trains Kadin," I explained. "They are speeding down the tracks and looking at the signs and reacting. Your train is just going faster than that of other people, so it's harder for you to see and read the signs."

"Uh huh," he replied.

I could see it all over his face that he was just tired of being in trouble all the time at school and at home.

My son was in the second grade, and his teacher, Ms. Rich, had called me in for a parent-teacher meeting.

As I walked into the school that warm September evening, I felt like I had been called to the principal's office. I felt sweat begin to drip down my back and I knew that my hands would be drenched when it was time to shake hands with her. I wiped my hands on my jeans and anxiously entered the classroom.

"Good evening Mrs. Addair, thank you so much for making the time to come in and speak with me." A petite, middle-aged yet stylishly dressed woman, Ms. Rich didn't seem too imposing as she directed me to be seated at a little desk and chair in front of the room.

"Let me start off by saying first that Kadin is a great kid, he is kind-hearted, and he wants to do well." Ms. Rich sat up straight in her chair behind her small desk. I looked around to see that the classroom was tidy and very colorful, inviting even. When I turned back to her she seemed a bit nervous herself, twirling a number two pencil around her fingers. She seemed to be choosing her words carefully, "He is struggling though because he has a hard time being still and keeping quiet. It's becoming a disruption in class."

I chewed my lower lip. "His previous teachers had the same problem and they recommended that we get him tested because they believe he has ADD if not ADHD."

"I have to agree." She nodded.

"But we really don't want to do that. They will only want to medicate him." I took a deep breath and exhaled. "Our nephew had terrible side effects from the medicine."

"There are different medicines now so they can help find out what works for him. I really do believe they will help." She looked me in the eyes boldly and stood, crossing her arms, and ended the conversation as if to say, "that's the answer and that's that." No longer was she trying to find the right words, instead it felt like the decision had been made and now I needed to leave.

Later that week, Kadin's pediatrician agreed. "Yes, he shows all the signs of ADD but I do not think that he suffers from ADHD."

"What's the difference?" I really had no idea about these disorders, but Kenny and I were very concerned about the side effects of the medicine that I'd heard about from friends who had kids with ADD.

"Essentially Kadin is struggling with keeping his mind still and focused so he is able to do what he needs to do. If he had ADHD, his whole body along with his mind would be unable to stay still," he explained.

"So that is like hyperactive?" I asked him.

"Yes, exactly." He didn't look up as he began writing out

the prescription for Kadin to start.

Kenny was not thrilled about medicating him, but we decided to trust the doctor and try to do everything we could to help Kadin. And so, the medication roller coaster began.

For the next two-and-a-half years we went through several different medications—Ritalin, Adderall, Adderall XL, and Concerta, rejecting one after another.

One of the medicines caused him to lose sixteen pounds in two months because he would hardly eat. Our seven-year-old son got to the point where he looked malnourished, and I couldn't stomach it any longer.

Another medicine made him so quiet that he held his little head down looking into his lap, hardly ever saying a word, constantly grinding his teeth.

The last straw was when he began having excruciating headaches with the third medicine and he seemed so doped up he wasn't even our child. Kadin's eyes would glaze over at the dinner table, and he'd stare at his partially eaten plate as if he didn't know where he was or why he was even sitting there. When his sister was being silly with French fries in her nose one night at the dinner table and he didn't even smile at her, I decided then that enough was enough.

I questioned the doctor, the teacher, and myself. These medicines are supposed to be helping my son?

We explained to Kadin, after several years of making him be a guinea pig for medications, he was going to have to try and do his best to be still and quiet in school…that this restless disorder was something he was going to have to live with for the rest of his life. We believed he needed to start recognizing his actions and correcting his behavior—that he should be able to do this on his own now because he was getting older.

"Kadin, you are ten years old, you are going to have to start to get control of yourself." Sitting down next to him on his bed, I looked around at the clothes and toys all over the floor and shook my head.

Kenny walked in. "Son, you are never going to get to ride your new dirt bike."

Ouch. My heart hurt for my son. My husband and I had got Kadin a dirt bike for Christmas and here it was mid-January and Kadin was still not allowed to ride it because he was punished every week.

Every Friday we got a report from Kadin's teacher, and it would determine if he was able to be free from restriction or if he would be punished for another weekend.

Kadin was grounded long and often because we were trying to get through to him. One day he came in from school, his face pale, dark circles under his eyes. Black crumbs lingered around his mouth that must have been left over from his Oreos at lunch.

"Hey, how was school Bud?" I asked, tired myself from cleaning the house and doing laundry, all day.

"Alright." He answered quietly, his shoulders slumped. He shuffled out of the kitchen, turning to go through the dining room into the adjoining living room.

"Anything fun or exciting to talk about?" I wiped the kitchen counter, listening for his reply.

Silence.

I walked into the living room to see his face and there he was curled up in the fetal position in his dad's chair, fast asleep. He had worked so hard all throughout the day at school to try and behave and get a good mark on his daily calendar that he was physically and mentally exhausted.

As I looked down at this precious kid, I could feel the hot tears streaming down my face. This kid who loved making us all smile and laugh, was himself doing anything but laughing and smiling. Our little people pleaser who always wanted to make everybody around him happy was failing miserably and it was weighing heavy on him. My heart ached for him, not for the first time, and I was sure not for the last.

Throughout his grade school years, Kadin played football, baseball, and wrestled. I think I pushed him into various sports because I wanted him to keep busy and stay out of trouble. As

I look back, I realize that I don't really know if playing all those sports was what he wanted to do. Did he enjoy playing the games? Did he like being on all those teams?

I know that if he didn't do well in academics or sports, he took it hard, and it upset him. Did my pushing him to play these sports do more harm than good to his self-esteem at his young age? Pushing and controlling is what I did best though. Kenny and I managed, coached, or volunteered in some way for all the after-school sports games that Kadin and Autumn participated in because we were dedicated to being in their lives. Later we realized we weren't really involved in their lives, sharing in what they were doing so much as we were busy being occupied by everything they were doing. Big difference.

Unfortunately for Kadin, he saw his sister Autumn do well in school, so to him I guess it looked like it was easy for her. It wasn't, but it must have seemed that way. I would explain that she worked as hard for her A as he did for his C, and we were proud of the effort not the letter. I don't think he really believed that. He would see all the praise that Autumn would get for her report card, and it must have been tough to take.

At every parent-teacher conference, the teacher always started with the same statement. "Kadin is a great kid, and he is really smart, he just won't be quiet." It was frustrating and after a while I think I became numb to their comments. When Kadin was fourteen, we moved to a new home, so he had to attend a different school. Since he had been with the same kids his entire childhood, I knew this was going to be hard for him, but I don't think I realized just how difficult it would be.

Kadin didn't make many friends his age at his new school. Instead, he constantly played video games by himself or would hang out with one of the older guys who worked for the party rental company we owned and operated and another who lived in the apartment above our garage.

Kadin withdrew from us, and school seemed even harder for him.

A little over two years later, Autumn went off to college

and suddenly, sixteen-year-old Kadin was alone. I remember the ride home from dropping her off—it was all about me, crying and feeling sorry for myself because my baby girl was gone. It took several weeks for me to finally ask Kadin if he missed his Sissy.

"Yeah, a little bit," he said, and I could see it in those doleful big brown eyes. I thought it was sweet that he missed his sister. It never occurred to me he was feeling more than just missing her.

What kind of mother am I? Why didn't I just take him for a burger or something when we dropped Autumn off and start a conversation and listen?

Kadin withdrew even further over the next couple years. He rarely came out of his room even to eat dinner. We could hear him talking to other players online on his X-Box but even then, he wasn't as animated anymore.

As a teenager, Kadin worked with us at our party rental business and he also had a job at a local restaurant in town, so he was always busy. There were times when he was hanging out with some of his old friends and sometimes the guys that worked for us after work, but we should really have had our eyes open to the fact that he was removing himself more and more from his father and I and our household. I would say to myself, he's just being a teenage boy who wants to hang out with his friends, not his parents. What we didn't realize was that new friends had entered Kadin's life and somehow, I missed finding out who they were until it was too late. It's ironic how controlling I was unless it was inconvenient for me.

I would look at him sometimes and ask, "Kadin, you doing okay?"

His standard answer was always, "Yeah, why?"

I could see in his eyes he really wasn't okay. He always seemed sad. But I shrugged it off, taking him at his word. I wasn't really sure how to talk with him about things, so it became easier to just ignore what I assumed were teenage mood swings.

Just after Kadin turned sixteen, he came to me and said, "Mom, I want to quit school." He leaned against the bathroom door frame, his shoulders drooped forward and his eyes pleading.

"Why Kadin?" I already knew the answer. But I can't help him quit, can I?

"I just don't want to keep doing this Mom, I don't do good in school and you know it!" His voice was trembling now.

"Well, we need to talk to Dad." I heard Kenny walking in the front door. Good timing.

We waited quietly as my husband trudged upstairs and saw us squared off, still in the bathroom doorway. "What's going on?" he asked, looking back and forth from Kadin to me.

"Go ahead." I nodded to our son.

"I want to quit school and get my GED." Kadin stood straighter, defiant in his tone.

"What did you say, Faith?" Kenny looked towards me, shocked.

"Well, I haven't said anything yet because I wanted to talk to you." I answered. "You know as well as I do that school is not his thing and he is struggling through it."

Kenny put his hands on his hips and shook his head, still in disbelief, then looked over at me again, defeat in his eyes. I could see he was tired of the fight too. Still, there was a trace of anger in his voice. "If you do this Kadin, I want you to get your GED right away and don't wait! And you will work full time, not stay home and lay around." His big arms folded across his chest to show he meant what he said.

"Okay." Kadin gave us a small smile and breathed a sigh of relief. "Thank you, Mom, Dad." He edged past us and walked down the stairs to his room.

I glanced at Kenny. His eyes were full of sadness, mirrors reflecting how I felt. I wondered if we had just done the right thing. But what was the right thing to do? I know it was the easier thing to do, for my husband and for me, but the right thing? I wasn't so sure.

A month later was GED test day. Kadin got up to leave early since he had to be at Rising Sun High School at seven-thirty a.m.

"Good luck!" I whispered loudly as he walked out the door. Kenny was still asleep upstairs.

"Thanks." He closed the door behind him.

Later that Saturday afternoon he walked into the house and before he could close the front door behind him, I was at the top of the steps of our bi-level home.

"Hey, how'd it go?" I asked, excited.

"I think I did good." He turned to close the front door and walk downstairs. I couldn't see his face which was shrouded by his raggedy black hoodie.

He headed down the six steps leading to his room. I watched as he trudged down each step, his feet looking as if sandbags were attached to his well-worn DC sneakers.

I nearly ran down the seven stairs to the foyer turning to following him down and into his bedroom, treading on his heels like an eager puppy dog. "You want something to eat? Or drink?" He never seems to look at me anymore, I thought.

"No, I'm going to lay down, I'm tired."

He gently closed the bedroom door. Hearing the click of the lock as I walked back upstairs and into the kitchen, I felt relieved that the test was done, yet still uneasy—about what I didn't know.

I had been looking forward to Easter weekend. Autumn would be home, and we would all be together as a family. I was really hoping that Kadin would liven up a little and act like our son again. I couldn't remember the last time he had made us laugh with something goofy that he did or told us. Wow, when was the last time? I wondered.

A few days later, we picked Autumn up from college and brought her home for the long holiday weekend.

Of course, she immediately went downstairs to her room.

"Hey Kadin," she said within earshot, then she turned right at the bottom of the steps and went to her room right across the narrow hall from Kadin's.

"Hey." I heard him answer.

As I went up the steps to sit down in my kitchen after the two-and-a-half-hour drive in the pouring rain, I laughed to myself. All this time she's been away from home and it's 'hey Kadin' and 'hey.' Teenagers!

Later that afternoon, I walked downstairs and paused at the bottom step, I could hear them talking softly but I couldn't make out what they were saying. But it didn't matter really because for a moment, all felt right and good in my world.

I walked towards her room and could hear them talking about Kadin's GED test that he just took. Kadin was saying he'd belatedly realized that he had misunderstood the explanation of one of the essay questions.

"I probably failed it." He looked up, startled, as I walked in, then hung his head, discouraged.

"So, you can just take it again." She said in that older sister, matter-of-fact way of hers as she was folding her clothes and putting them away in her dresser. Her lightened brown hair, in a messy ponytail, was still slightly wet from a shower and the fact she wore no makeup didn't take away from how beautiful she looked. Her sweet round cheeks, which I have never been able to keep from pinching, glowed with happiness. She's happy to be home.

"Yeah, I guess I can." Kadin mumbled back, standing up, turning his back and walking past me to his room across the hall, softly closing the door behind him. Click.

In stark contrast to his sister, he was gaunt and thinner than ever, his shoulders drooping in his dingy tee-shirt and faded jeans. His thin face looked gray and tired.

Autumn looked at me, unasked questions in her big brown eyes. I simply shook my head not able to give any answers. I walked out of her room and back upstairs and into the kitchen, opening the freezer door staring through the frozen fog of steam that floated out, wondering what would I cook tonight for dinner…and what was going on with Kadin.

A few weeks later Kadin received a letter in the mail that said he needed to retake the essay part of the test. I scheduled the test time for him for a little over two weeks away.

I wasn't home the afternoon he went in to take the test because I was coordinating a wedding for our event company, but I called him.

"Hello?" It came out in a slurred whisper.

"Whoa, did I wake you up?"

His voice sounded like sandpaper sliding across wood. "Yeah, I was tired."

"Wow, you do sound tired, are you feeling, okay?"

"Yeah, I'm just tired Mom."

"Okay, well how did you do?" I put my finger in my other ear trying to hear over the metal chairs clanging and tables banging in the party tent behind me. I turned to glare at the culprits, two gangly teens who were just doing their jobs, trying to silence them with my stare but they didn't even notice me.

"I did good, I think I passed it."

"Yay!" I cheered.

"Okay, I'm gonna get off here, love you."

"Love you too baby, I'm so proud of you."

"Thanks, love you." The phone went silent.

I went back to work, but it was hard to focus. I started yelling at the two young guys to try to keep the racket down, and then felt guilty and apologized. I felt tears sting my eyes, my emotions all over the place. Something is going on with my son, but I have no idea what it is. I started putting the linens on the tables but I felt so on edge that I caught myself barking orders at the guys again like a boot camp drill sergeant.

I went over to the restroom trailer, went inside and sat on the lid of one of the toilets. I sat there for a few minutes with my face on my knees, hot tears dripping from my eyes and plopping on the floor at my feet.

Lord, I prayed quietly, something is going on with Kadin and I am freaking out here. I don't know what it is and I don't know how to help him. Help me to figure out what to do. Amen.

Walking to the sink and mirror, a lady walked in as I splashed water on my face. I was washing the tears away and cleaning up my runny nose.

"Are you okay?" she looked at me with concern.

"Oh yes," I groaned, "These allergies are going to be the death of me."

"Oh you're not kidding," she sounded relieved. "My son has terrible allergies and it took us months to figure out what to do for him." She walked into a stall.

"Have a great time today." I called back to her as I rushed out of the restroom like I was being chased by a rabid dog.

"You ..." I didn't hear the rest of her reply.

About a month later, as Kadin and I were headed home from work, we stopped at the mailbox before driving up to the house. I pulled out a big manilla envelope and I could just tell...there it was, his GED!

"Get out!" I yelled at him excitedly, flapping the envelope in his face, waking him from dozing against the passenger door.

"What?" He looked at me with bleary eyes, alarmed.

"Get out, I want to take your picture getting your GED!"

"Geez mom." He waved his arm in the air towards me as if to ward off my attack.

I put the truck in park and made Kadin get out to re-enact the scene, telling him to re-open the mailbox and then pose with the envelope, then with the diploma he pulled out.

All the while he was grumbling that he didn't want to take any pictures and that he didn't feel good.

But I ignored him, insisting on "just one more" pose with his new diploma.

"Come on Mom, I just want to get in and lay down." He frowned at me and I yelled at him to smile, holding up the phone. I said, "it's not going to kill you to let me take your picture, I'm proud of you.".

Wow, he looks like he hasn't slept in a week. I hope he isn't getting sick. I thought, taking one last photo, and then lowering my phone. "Go ahead." I waved my hand at him and watched him slowly walk up the driveway and into the house. His royal blue North East Indians hoodie hung down from his shoulders looking five sizes too big. He likes his clothes baggy, I thought, but wow. I'll just check on him later.

Later that evening, gazing blindly out the kitchen window while I stirred the gravy for dinner, my mind ran in a million different places. Work was crazy, the house was a mess, and Kadin wasn't acting like himself. Chaos—my life was in chaos. A few minutes later, leaning over the steps, I called out,

"Kadin, it's time for dinner, come on up and eat." No answer.

"Kadin!" Nothing.

I walked down the steps to his bedroom and opened his door. I heard a soft tinkle, and looking down I saw a little bell hanging from the door knob. Funny, I'd never noticed it before. I continued into his room towards his bed.

"Kadin," I touched his shoulder. He didn't respond.

I shook him a little harder, "Kadin, it's dinner time." Nothing.

"Kadin!" My voice sounded annoyingly loud in my own ears.

"What?" He grumbled.

"It is time for dinner!" I barked like a drill sergeant.

"I'm not hungry." He snapped back at me as he rolled over in his bed away from me.

I realized my entire body was rigid.

Trying to relax my clenched jaw, I put dinner on my plate and walked into the living room and sat down, my dinner getting cold as I mindlessly stared at "Wheel of Fortune" on the television set.

Tossing and turning in bed that night, sleep wouldn't come. I got up at about three a.m. and quietly walked out of our bedroom, softly closing the door behind me.

I walked down the steps to Kadin's bedroom and opened his door, the bell tinkling to announce my entrance.

He was sleeping soundly so I turned and walked out of his room, closing the door behind me, the little bell seeming to ring even louder behind me.

I made it to the top of the steps before I burst out in tears. I sat there on the landing, crying and praying, filled with sorrow. I felt like I was grieving for my son and feeling like things couldn't possibly get any worse.

I didn't know that his situation was going to get a lot worse and we would deal with fear and grief far greater than we could ever have imagined.

CHAPTER THREE

WAKE UP CALL

Kadin had just turned eighteen and was invited to spend the weekend with a "friend" and her parents in Virginia. This was the first time we had heard of this girl, so I arranged to meet with her mother and the young lady before we agreed to him going.

As Ann and her mother drove up our driveway in a nice, dark-green, four-door sedan, Kadin seemed excited, maybe even nervous. He was talking a mile a minute and he couldn't seem to stand still. He'd also gotten a haircut, and was dressed in dark blue polo shirt and jeans. I thought to myself that he looked so handsome and happy.

Ann's mom Patricia and I talked outside, and she told me that they had a cabin in Virginia and her husband would be joining them on Friday night.

"Ann gets bored because there really isn't much to do there so when she asked for Kadin to come, I was happy he was interested in making the trip."

I felt frumpy standing next to Patricia, her petite, five-foot-two figure sheathed in expensive charcoal gray slacks and a light pink silk blouse. Not one strand of her golden-auburn hair was out of place and her small heart-shaped face glowed with expertly applied make up.

"We will pick Kadin up on Friday morning about eleven o'clock and we will have him home sometime late afternoon or early evening on Sunday if that is okay with you?" Patricia's bright green eyes bore into me, expecting an answer.

"That will be fine.' I assured her.

"We have plenty of room so he will have a room of his own and he doesn't need to bring anything special other than clothes and a little spending money. We'll be eating at the cabin mostly but if we do stop on the road, he'll need to be ready for that too."

I looked over at Kadin and Ann by the back deck. My son was leaning down talking to Ann since she was barely five-foot tall including the huge pair of white sunglasses on the top of her head. Ann's wavy light brown hair was tousled from the wind but managed to look stylish rather than messy. Her beautiful white smile flashed up at Kadin and the sound of her laugh reminded me of the wind chimes hanging from the trees in our backyard.

I guess he'll be okay, I thought, forcing myself to stay positive.

Kadin came home from the trip and seemed to be very happy and relaxed.

"Did you have fun?" I asked as we drove to Walmart to get groceries.

"Yeah, it was nice there."

"What did you guys do?"

"Nothing really, we played some cards and watched television." Texting on his phone, he didn't even look up when he answered me.

"Was her family nice?"

"Yeah, they were nice. Didn't see her dad too much though."

About a week later Kadin came to me asking, "Mom, can

Ann stay with us a couple days? Her mom kicked her out of the house."

"Why did she kick her out?" I asked him.

"I'm not really sure but she said that she and her mom always argue because she is adopted." He leaned back against the kitchen counter, crossed his long legs and gripped the countertop behind him.

Mulling it over, I couldn't think of anything that made me feel uncomfortable or that gave me the "uh oh" feeling. "Okay Kadin, yes for a couple days." I hoped my husband would be in agreement. Oh well, he isn't here to help me decide, I reasoned.

For the next few days, Ann cleaned our house from top to bottom. When I came home from work the very first day I was flabbergasted, looking around at the clean countertops and sparkling appliances. I found our house guest in the living room, dusting. "Thank you so much but you didn't have to clean up the kitchen."

She grinned, her smile dazzling, her green eyes sparkling, and flip her long light-brown hair behind her. She was a pretty young girl. "I just wanted you to know how grateful I was that you're letting me stay here and feeding me and stuff." Her face, while tan and healthy, was very thin and I felt sorry for her.

"Sure, no problem." I guess I could talk Kenny into letting her stay a few more days.

Since 2004 I have had some pretty serious medical issues with Arnold Chiari Malformation and Syringomyelia but have never had any pain medicine in the house until I tore my rotator cuff in my shoulder about six weeks before Kadin went away with Ann and her mom. I didn't take the medicine much because it made me so tired, but it never occurred to me, at any point, to keep track of my medicine to make sure none was missing. I certainly never thought that it would be stolen and abused.

One afternoon Kadin said he and Ann were going to run to Walmart to get a few things she needed like shampoo and bodywash. Kenny and I were sitting at home watching TV and relaxing with our three dogs.

A few hours later Ann called. "I don't know where Kadin is and my stuff is in his truck …" Something in her voice made me sit up straight. I could hear something in her voice…fear.

"Wait, what do you mean you don't know where he is Ann? You left with him a little bit ago, where did you go?" I asked her.

"We went to Walmart, but then we split up and I can't find him and he has his keys and I need my stuff." Her words tumbled out so fast I had to strain to hear what she was saying.

"Okay Ann, where is Kadin? What is going on?" I could hear my tone get a little louder and sharper, but I didn't care. I was standing now, pacing with the phone in my hand.

"What's going on?" Kenny leaned forward in his chair.

I put my hand over the receiver end of the phone. "I'm not sure, Ann said she doesn't know where Kadin is." I took another deep breath, trying to keep it together.

"Ann, where are you?" I asked.

"Wal-Mart" she answered, "in the parking lot."

"Ok, we will be right there." I hung up and gathered my purse and keys.

"What's going on?" Kenny asked again, annoyed.

"I don't know, and she's not saying so we have to go figure it out." I spouted.

Slamming our way out the front door, we rushed to our truck not knowing we were headed for a storm—or maybe a hurricane.

The fifteen-minute drive to the Northeast Plaza felt like it took an hour. Both Kenny and I spit questions back and forth to each other but neither of us had any answers.

We tried calling his cell phone on the way to find him, but there was no answer.

What is going on? my mind screamed. I was terrified of what I had no idea. Is he okay? My heart was racing, and I felt like I was gulping for air. Oh God please, I prayed quietly.

When we finally pulled up next to Kadin's truck, Ann stood

there in the parking lot next to it waiting for us. Her thin arms were crossed, her eyes squinted against the early evening setting sun. She was clearly perturbed. We both got out of the truck and approached her, but she stepped back like a wary animal.

"Do you have a key? I need to get my stuff!" The hardened, angry look in her eyes startled me. This was not the same young lady who had been in our home for the last couple of days.

"No, we don't, and you need to help us figure out what's going on. What happened? When did you last see Kadin?" I shot questions at her like a deputy at a murder scene investigation. I wanted answers and I wanted them now!

"All I know is he might have got stopped by some workers in Walmart because they said we were stealing stuff. And then the cops came and might have arrested him." She told us all of this nonchalantly, as if we were taking up her time. She was being evasive, but she knew what happened, we could see it on her face.

"Stealing stuff? What stuff? Cops? What cops?" I was shouting at her.

"Did the police take Kadin somewhere Ann?" Kenny asked with a patience that made me want to scream, how can you be so calm right now?

"Yeah." She answered simply, arms crossed across her chest.

"Which police?" he asked her calmly.

"I think the state maybe." She answered. After almost thirty minutes talking in the parking lot, we finally got this little bit of information from her.

"Okay, we are going to go over there and see what's going on." Kenny said to me as we turned back towards our truck.

"I'm going to need a ride." Ann said, as if we should know this and jump to help her out.

"Okay, but my husband and I are going to the police station so you will have to wait in the truck until we are done talking to them if you want a ride from us." I stated flatly.

"Okay." She opened the back door and hopped into our

truck like we were going for a joy ride.

"Wow." I was infuriated.

Both Kenny and I asked her over and over, "What happened Ann, we just need to know something, anything so we're not in the dark."

But she remained aloof. "I don't know, I'm not sure," she kept answering, as annoyed with us as we were with her. Begging did no good. She was absolutely no help.

She knows what happened. How dare she not tell us? I wanted to make Kenny stop the truck so I could yank her out and shake the truth out of her!

The two-minute drive to the Maryland State Police barracks was tense, to say the least.

Walking into the station, my mind was going in a million directions. What are we doing here? This is our son, this is not happening. The dim entryway was not welcoming or comforting.

As I approached the front desk, the burly female officer slowly slid the huge glass window aside. "Can I help you?"

"Yes ma'am, we are looking for our son Kadin Addair." I paused and then continued. "We were told he was picked up about an hour ago." Even to me my voice sounded whiny and pleading.

"One moment." She closed the heavy glass door. I could hear my heart pounding in my ears while I waited in the silence of the lobby.

Opening the glass door and without taking her hand off it, she said "Yes ma'am, he's here."

"Can you tell me why?" I asked before she could slide the door closed again.

Looking back down at her desk she replied, "No ma'am, he is eighteen years old so you will have to wait until an officer comes out to speak with you."

"Do you know how long that will be?" I tried to make eye contact with her. Surely, she could see how worried I was and would want to help us.

"No ma'am I do not." She slid the glass door closed, it's

loud bang sounding, to me, like a jail cell slamming.

AHHHHHHH! My mind was screeching. I cannot handle this. I need to be able to figure out how to fix this. Kadin has never been in trouble before. We can fix this.

After an hour sitting in the waiting area, two officers finally walked in the entrance into the lobby where we sat. One said to the other, "…yeah he had several guns when we picked him up, the guns are still in my trunk." They continued through a set of doors into the back, not realizing that Kenny and I had stopped breathing. The metal door closed behind them, echoing loudly through the waiting area.

"Oh my God," I said in shock.

"We don't know that was about him so just relax." Kenny said.

But we were anything but relaxed.

Almost four hours later Kadin was brought out into the waiting area in handcuffs.

"Oh God." I said aloud. My son looked terrified.

As we stood up the officer said, "Folks I am taking him to the Commissioner's office at the Courthouse, you can meet us there."

"What is going on Kadin?" I asked him but he wouldn't look me in the eye.

"Ma'am, you cannot talk to him right now."

"He's our son!" I cried.

"He's an adult Ma'am." The officer walked out the front doors of the barracks, taking Kadin in handcuffs with him.

"Good luck." The muffled parting words of the officer could be heard from behind the glass door at the reception desk.

We were still no closer to knowing what was going on, so the ten-minute ride from North East to the District Courthouse in Elkton was excruciating. At this point Kenny and I were so nervous and scared that we were just snapping at one another, blaming each other for not being aware of what was going on or what could be happening, even though neither of us had a clue at this point.

Meanwhile, Ann was in the back seat sleeping. Sleeping!

Like she didn't have a care in the world.

I kept telling myself once we knew what we were dealing with, we'd be able to fix it and Kadin would be alright, and all would be okay in our world again. The unknown was what was so scary, and I was not comfortable because I felt like I had absolutely no control over this entire situation. Our eyes were opened though once we walked into the big brick courthouse on Main Street and then into the Commissioner's office. The cramped little room was packed wall to wall with alleged criminals, which now included our son. At first, all my clouded mind could think was, I didn't know the courthouse was open at eleven-thirty at night. The officer with Kadin told us we could talk to our son now.

"What's going on Kadin?" I demanded, wanting to hear what I needed to fix.

His body slumped down in the chair as if he was trying to make himself as small as possible. "I got arrested for shoplifting at Walmart." Kadin spoke in a deadpan voice, showing no emotion. His face was colorless, except for the dark gray circles still under his blank eyes.

Thank God. My mind relaxed for a moment because he wasn't in trouble for the guns the police officers were talking about at the station earlier.

Looking at Kadin I knew something else was going on because he wouldn't make eye contact with me. I looked from Kadin to the officer, who said, "Actually, he was detained for suspicion of shoplifting but he was arrested for possession of heroin."

I could feel the air forcing its way out of my lungs as I choked back, "WHAT? Heroin?" My voice came out in a high-pitched squeak. I sounded irrational, even to my own ears.

"I found it on the ground, and I picked it up and put it in my pocket." As Kadin told us the lie, the officer shook his head.

"Come on man," the officer said to Kadin, then turned to Kenny and I. "I don't believe that and besides it doesn't matter, he had enough on him to be charged with distribution."

I could feel Kenny's body tense up next to me. I turned

and looked at him, his gray eyes filled with…what? Fear? Anger? His typically ruddy, handsome face looked like the blood had drained from it only to slowly rush back in, making even the part in his light-brown hair turn red.

"Kadin, what were you doing with heroin?" I whispered the last word. I didn't want to hear his answer, but it was too late to take back the question.

This can't be real. Heroin? My mind screamed in disbelief and fear. No, this isn't real. I immediately began making excuses. This is Ann's doing, it's her drugs. This is not how we raised Kadin. He has no need for drugs! I continued to rant on to myself.

But when I looked at Kadin, searched his face and eyes, those guilty sad eyes, I knew. Our son was arrested for drugs because he'd been using them.

I looked around the room as one of the overhead fluorescent lights flickered and saw another kid, probably about Kadin's age, slumped over sideways in the chair slapping his thigh to a beat only he could hear.

There were way too many people in here. I suddenly felt claustrophobic my anxiety rising and the roaring in my ears growing louder, deafening. My stomach turned and I thought I was going to get sick right there on the floor, but somehow, I managed not to.

As I looked over at Kenny, I noticed how scared he was, but I could also see that he was really angry. His arms crossed his chest and his entire upper body was rigid and straight while I felt like mine was quickly wilting like a dandelion out of water.

Kadin was taken to see the commissioner and we waited an interminable hour for the verdict.

I felt relieved when the officer came out and told us that Kadin was either going to jail or we could pay his bail to get him out tonight.

"Let him stay in jail." My husband's statement sucked the air out of the room with its finality.

"NO!" I hissed at him. "I am not going to let him stay in jail." *I gotta save him.*

My mind raced now. Do I have enough cash on me to pay his bail? I've got to help him get out of here. My maternal instincts won over. We quickly dashed to the closest ATM then went back to pay the required five hundred dollars in bail and they released Kadin.

We headed back to Kadin's truck in the Wal-Mart parking lot, all four of us silent the entire drive. Ann never stirred from her blissful, drug-induced sleep.

Kenny picked up Kadin's truck then rode home with him and I drove home with Ann still sleeping in the back seat of my truck.

Autumn was at the house when we got home. She had switched to attending a college close to home now. She was livid. She walked downstairs and made Ann get her things together.

"Nope." I heard our quiet daughter say loudly. "That is Kadin's not yours, nice try. A few seconds later, I heard her shout, "get your crap and hurry up!"

Finally, I heard Autumn yell, "Mom we're ready!" Then the front door slammed.

I got into the truck and the tension was so thick I had to roll down the window to feel like I could breathe.

"Where to?" I asked Ann.

"I don't know, I guess Elkton." She huffed.

The fifteen minutes it took to drive from our house to Elkton was filled with her talking to herself.

"What am I supposed to do now?" She asked nobody in particular but seemed to expect an answer. With a loud dramatic sigh, she dialed her phone and whined into it, "Hey, can I come over? I don't know, just a little while I guess."

"Where are we taking you?" I asked her.

"I'm trying to find out now!" she snapped back at me.

"HEY!" Autumn turned around in the front seat to look at Ann in the back. "You better be really careful right now." Her voice was quiet, but her tone was menacing.

I reached over to put my hand on Autumn's leg to try and calm her down.

"Tell us where to take you or we will drop you off right here." Autumn turned back around in her seat. She was done. "Just take me to the Manor." She hissed snidely, referring to the neighborhood across from the county jail, known for its population of criminals, crack addicts and drug dealers.

Great, I thought sarcastically. Just where I want to be with my daughter—the drug infested projects in the middle of the night.

I pulled into the neighborhood and eased the truck over to the shoulder.

"No, I need to go down to the first road and turn right." she demanded.

I felt my teeth sinking into my bottom lip as I followed her instructions and made the turn.

"Here ya' go, take care." I pulled over again in front of a small rundown house. The wooden fence surrounding it was missing more slats than it had holding it up and the gate falling forward off its hinges as if it had been holding the weight of the world on its thin wooden frame.

"Wow, really?" She jerked her bags out onto the road and slammed the door so hard we could hear the windows vibrate.

I put the truck in reverse, locked the doors and peeled out, the tires screeching. I looked in my rearview mirror as we pulled away and saw Ann standing in the road screaming at us and giving us the middle finger.

"Unbelievable," Autumn shook her head, "she is crazy."

We headed back home in silence.

I never asked about the conversation Kenny and Kadin had that night as they drove home. I know that it was hard, but I didn't ask because I really wasn't ready to hear the truth from either of them yet.

CHAPTER FOUR

REHAB

As we sat in the living room that night facing each other, Kadin did most of the talking. He was saying all the right things.

"I'm sorry Mom, Dad I didn't mean for this to happen." He looked at me and then Kenny, leaning forward from his father's tan recliner.

"You have to quit Kadin," Kenny said sternly. He sat back in the armchair closest to Kadin.

"Don't you think I want to Dad? Don't you think I've tried?" His eyes darted back and forth between us, begging us to understand.

"I throw my guts up because I've tried to stop, and it makes me so sick. Mom," Kadin went on, "I'm sorry, I just don't know what to do."

"I know," I told him, but as I looked at him from the couch across the living room, I felt like at that moment I didn't know anything anymore.

Guilt, anger, fear, blame, denial—the list went on of the emotions we felt the first few days after Kadin's arrest for possession of heroin.

Just a few days later we called a dear friend, Phil Meekins, who was a recovering addict himself and the pastor of one of the local churches. More importantly, Pastor Phil ministered to, or "loved on," as he called it, local people who were stricken with poverty, sickness, addiction or whatever else it was that brought a person down to their "bottom." At that time, he had just over twenty years clean and sober himself and he was happy to share that with those he helped.

"Phil, my friend," I said into the phone.

"Hey, my sister," he said, as he always called me, "talk to me, what's going on?" He must have heard something in my voice that made him aware that something was wrong.

"Phil, we need help for Kadin. He got into some trouble, and we found out that he has been using drugs."

"Alright, what is he using, do you know?" he asked matter-of-factly. Pastor Phil was already on the case.

"He's told us heroin and K-2, you know that spice stuff, fake marijuana, have you heard of that?" I asked. We sure had never heard of it before now, but our vocabulary was beginning to grow in ways I wished it wouldn't.

"Yeah, I know it," he growled with his slightly southern drawl. "That stuff is no good, but then again, none of it is."

"What do we do Phil? We are so scared, and Kenny and I just don't know where to start."

"Come on over to the house tonight and we will talk about it, bring Kadin with you."

I wasn't sure what to expect when we got to his house, but Phil was just…Phil. He walked out of the sprawling brick rancher surrounded by nothing but trees, looking fresh from a shower. His shoulder length brown wavy hair was slightly damp, his beard, streaked with the beginnings of gray, was dry and freshly brushed.

"Hey, my friends!" His big voice reached us easily across the sixty or so feet to our truck in the gravel driveway. "Come on out and talk with me a little bit." He waved us over nonchalantly to join him in the front yard, as if we were coming for a barbeque.

As we walked toward him, I couldn't help but look at him

and wonder how in the world he could have his sleeves rolled up, almost to his elbows, on this chilly night in December.

"Come here Sis," he reached out to me with those tattooed arms and hugged me.

We stood in his front yard while Phil loved on us for a few minutes. As he explained the recovery process I began to feel like *Okay, everything is really going to be good.*

"I made a call to a place in North Carolina that I've just started to help support and they said that they will talk to Kadin." He put his arm around my son, who appeared ready and willing, at least for the moment, to hear what Phil had to say.

"North Carolina?" Kenny and I both asked. "Why so far away?

"Because that is where he needs to go to get clean. He needs to be away from the people he has been hanging around with and the places that he frequents." Phil explained patiently.

"Yeah, but so far?" I asked again.

"Faith, you are going to have to realize this is serious." His eyes bore into mine. "He is going to lie and manipulate you any way he can to get what he wants, which right now is drugs." Kadin's face flushed red, and he bowed his head, looking guiltily down at his feet.

I was taken aback. *No! Kadin is a good kid who just made some poor choices.* I shook my head but before I could speak, Phil saw my distress and cut me off.

"I love Kadin and y'all are like family to me, so I am going to say it to you straight. If you do not take this seriously and make him accountable, you will lose him. This has to be his choice, his decision. Are you hearing me?" He leaned toward us for emphasis. "Kadin got himself here, he has to choose to get himself out."

After just a few seconds I asked quietly, "Okay, how do we start?"

"Here is the phone number," Phil handed Kadin a piece of

paper. "Call them and tell them who you are. They will ask you a few questions, but you will have to fill out an application for them to consider you, then they'll interview you. They will expect you to have any legal problems settled and you'll have to get tests for HIV and hepatitis before you can go in also."

Oh my God, my mind screamed, *HIV? Hepatitis? This can't be happening, it can't be real.* Oh, but it was.

The days following were not easy for Kadin or for the rest of us. Clearly, he was not feeling well and was more than a little grumpy and anxious. He was sick and hurting and edgy. Meanwhile I had to help him get all the forms filled out and the tests done without letting him out of my sight because Phil had already warned us, "He will use again right now if he can find a way."

"We will just tell people that you are going away to school, like a trade school," I said in desperation as the three of us sat in the living room talking again a few nights later.

"What? No!" Kenny said. "We can't lie, Faith, why would we lie?" My husband looked at me like I was going crazy. Maybe I was.

"I don't know, I just don't want people to think badly about Kadin." I guess I was worried about what people were going to think about our son—but deep down I knew I was even more concerned about what they were going to think of me and what kind of mother I was and how I had failed him. Why is it I wasn't worried what people would think about Kenny—whether he was a bad dad? Which he was not, but it is odd that it never crossed my mind that he would be looked at as having failed at parenting too.

Still, the lies were swarming around in my head like a hive of angry bees. I was not really understanding the seriousness of the situation yet. I think I was in denial. In my mind we were going to get Kadin help and he would be okay. As long as I could figure out how we could fix him without people knowing what was going on so they wouldn't find out what a bad mother I was, everything would be alright. Talk about walking a tightrope…I was frantic, my hands shaking and sweat breaking out on my forehead, my mind was racing.

"Okay." I'm not sure if I was agreeing not to lie, or saying what my husband wanted to hear, wishing it would all just go away.

The phone call finally came almost two weeks later. Greg from Redeemer Recovery, the Christian rehab and recovery center in North Carolina, spoke to Kadin for a while and told him they would take him—as to when, we didn't know yet.

"What did he say? What was he asking, Kadin?" I needed to try to find out as much information as possible.

He stood up from his bed, unstable. "I don't know, Mom, they just asked a bunch of questions." His voice trailed as he started to walk out of his room and upstairs.

I got up from his bed and followed him upstairs and into the kitchen.

"Kadin, it will all be okay once you get down there. They are going to help you." I think I was comforting myself as much as I was trying to reassure our son. Honestly, I had no idea what they were going to do; I just knew that he needed to go— convinced now by Phil that there was no other option.

Basically, the rehab people told us we had to wait another three more weeks before we could get him down to North Carolina. *Three more weeks.* I wasn't sure I'd make it. My mind was tired. I was tired. *How are we going to make it three more weeks?* Kadin seemed relieved, I guess he was tired too. The dark circles around his eyes were more noticeable now than ever before. I had to laugh at myself and my ignorance. I know now the dark circles weren't from my son staying up too late at night playing on his Xbox.

"I told you!" Autumn yelled into my ear through the cell phone. Our daughter and her boyfriend Calvin were doing some Christmas shopping and Kadin apparently asked to tag along. "I told you, Mom." Her anger dissipated as she talked. Now she just sounded sad.

"What? What's going on?" I asked, but I knew already.

"We ran into the store and Kadin said he would wait in the car and when we came out, he was gone."

"Where could he have gone?" I asked.

"I don't know Mom," she huffed "but I know why!"

"Drive around and see if you can find him please." I could already feel the panic building up inside me like a pressure cooker.

A few minutes stretched by before she called me back. "He's here with us." She sounded frustrated and angry again. "I'm bringing him back. He said he went to pee in the woods but that is a lie!"

A half hour later her familiar small blue Chevy pulled into our drive.

"Thank you, guys," I said to Autumn and Calvin when they brought Kadin into the house, one on each side of him, as if they were guards and he was an inmate.

My daughter was scowling, clearly not happy with her brother, and she wanted me to know it. "He can't be trusted right now Mom. He's trying to get drugs. He probably already got some."

"We will just have to keep an eye on him until he goes away," I said sadly, realizing I had lost control. *What more can I do?*

I watched in disbelief as he shook away his bodyguards, stormed down the stairs and slammed his bedroom door behind him.

Autumn stomped up the steps and into the kitchen, mumbling in her anger. The sound of cabinet doors being opened and closed could be heard throughout the house.

Later that afternoon when we had all settled down and I was starting to prepare dinner, Kadin had the nerve to tell us he was frustrated with all of us when he walked into the kitchen. I tried to wrap my mind around the irony in this.

"You all need to chill out and trust me," he snapped

defensively. "I wasn't doing anything." He turned and opened the refrigerator.

"Kadin, your sister was scared and worried about you, so were Dad and I."

"Like I said, I wasn't doing anything wrong." He looked at me as he walked back out of the kitchen.

When did his eyes start looking at me with lies in them? When did I begin to believe them? *Oh my God, hurry!* I silently pleaded for three weeks to be over so we could finally get him in rehab.

That night I walked downstairs to check on him. As I walked into his room I saw a small palm size, pipe-like glass "bowl" on his nightstand. I knew it was used for smoking pot or K-2.

"Kadin!" I said through gritted teeth as I shoved his shoulder to wake him. He just continued to sleep with no more than a grunt. I picked up the bowl and dropped it into the half full cup of orange soda next to it.

I was angry at myself for almost believing him.

All the health tests were done and Kadin was cleared for acceptance. Almost a week later, Kadin went to court for the charges he had been arrested for. Because he was going to rehab and he had never been in trouble before this, the judge dropped the charges. Kadin was one step closer to getting his life back.

We started the trip to take Kadin to rehab, three weeks later, very early the following Saturday morning— four a.m. to be exact. The eight-hour drive to Lenoir, North Carolina was not a happy affair. Watching the scenery fly by as I looked out my window on that February morning, I realized it looked exactly how I felt—cold, barren, not living, just there. Kadin slept most of the way and Kenny and I just didn't have much to say. *Thank God for the radio.*

Walking in the front door of Redeemer that day was an eye opener, although I'm not sure what I was expecting. The old brown paneling on every wall made the office area feel even darker and more cramped than it already was. The smell reminded me of my great grandmother's house, that musty basement smell that isn't gross but not pleasant either. Every step that we took inside made the floor creak and moan as if it was sympathizing with our pain. The dark carpet on the floor was well worn by the many feet that had walked through those doors. We were greeted as if we were there for a doctor's appointment.

"Name?" The man behind the counter asked.

"Kadin Addair." I said as I stepped forward, feeling like a robot. I looked up at him. He stood over six feet tall and his short dark hair was neatly cut. He was about thirty-five-years old and I later found out that he was a former resident of Redeemer and a recovering addict himself.

"Kadin Addair?" The man flipped through his papers on his clipboard. "Kadin?" he asked, looking past me to my son.

"Yeah," Kadin responded quietly as he stepped forward.

"Come with me," the man said as he turned and started walking away. "You need to say goodbye to your parents now," he added gruffly over his shoulder.

Kadin was immediately ushered further back into the office, his bags taken from him. Questions were shot at him as he was told to empty his pockets onto the counter.

Kenny and I just quietly watched until I couldn't stand the silence. "We were going to stay just for a few minutes to get him settled…"

"No ma'am," the man shook his head. "We got him from here, safe travels home." He turned away from us with a dismissive wave and then back to Kadin, shielding him from our view as they retreated away from us.

"Okay Kadin, do you have any drugs on you right now?" I heard the man ask. I didn't hear Kadin's reply but the last thing I heard was, "so if I pee test you right now will you have drugs in your system?

CHAPTER FIVE

RELAPSE

"I'm not gonna make it Mom." His voice sounded tired, sad and a million miles away instead of the five hundred it actually was.

"Yes, you are Kadin," I answered quietly back into the phone. "You got this. It's only been a week."

"You don't understand, it sucks here! The food is terrible...for breakfast we had cereal they call the Redeemer mix because it's like eight different types of cereal all mixed up."

"Okay, well you love cereal Kadin," I said in the most reassuring tone I could muster.

"Mom, they mix in warm water to thin down soy milk." I was quiet for a few seconds, "Mom? Are you still there?" he asked.

"Yeah, I'm here buddy," I cleared my throat. "I was just trying to think of something to say but I got nothing. That sounds gross." I snickered, trying to keep it light.

"It is. And for lunch we had a sandwich with one piece of bologna, no cheese, and one guy found some mold on his bread." He sounded annoyed.

"Well, Kadin you just have to stay strong and don't let things like that drive you crazy, okay? Dad and I are praying for you, we love you and we are very proud of you for doing what you have to do to get well so hang in there okay?" I kept talking, trying to fill in the time so that I didn't have to hear how miserable he was.

After I hung up, I was sobbing as I told Kenny about our conversation, "He is going to starve to death. I don't understand why they don't give them better food. It would make it so much easier for him to concentrate on getting clean." I whined through my snotty nose.

Kenny pulled me into his safe, strong arms and hugged me. "Just look at it this way, I bet he is going to have a whole new appreciation for your pot roast and meatloaf." I could feel my tenseness ease a bit as we both had a little chuckle over that. Our picky eater was not going to have an easy time of it but maybe that would be a deterrent for ever going back.

Over the next couple of weeks, Kadin would call and sometimes he would sound like he was depressed, and then other times he would call and say what a great church service they had. One night he called at his usual eight-thirty p.m. and the sound of his voice was soft and peaceful and yet excited.

"Mom, get a piece of paper and a pencil, you got to write these songs down," he said. "They are awesome, '10,000 Reasons' and 'Hosanna' by Starfield, these are amazing Mom, guys were praising and crying and stuff in chapel tonight, it was awesome." He finished, sounding breathless.

"Wow, that is so great Kadin," I looked over to Kenny sitting across from me in the living room. We were both listening on speakerphone and smiled at each other knowingly—we were not surprised that it was music that brought our son back to the Lord because we both knew music spoke to him.

"We are so proud of you Kadin!" Kenny yelled at the phone from his recliner.

"Thanks," he said. "So, I've decided to do the sixty-five-day program instead of the thirty-day because I think it will work better for me."

Kenny and I hesitated for a moment and then my husband said, "Well you know that will go into the beginning of our busy season." I knew he was a little aggravated. We relied heavily on Kadin for our rental business to run a crew and without him, we were down a driver and crew leader.

"I know Dad, but I have to do this." Kadin's excitement seemed to be disappearing now like cool water being poured onto a campfire.

"You do what you got to do, Kadin." Kenny still sounded perturbed, clearly not agreeing with our son's decision. Kenny is old school and believes that you don't miss work for anything, and this was unacceptable to him. I knew he still subconsciously believed that Kadin should be able to man up and stop doing drugs. Neither of us understood how hard this was going to be.

After I hung up, I was aggravated with Kenny because I felt like he had been too hard on Kadin.

I quietly put on my pajamas, trying to hold my tongue but my temper won out. I folded my arms across my chest, glaring at my husband. "I wish you would have encouraged him and left it at that."

"You can't keep babying him, Faith." Kenny sighed and laid on the bed, picking up his Robert Jordan paperback.

"I'm not!"

"Yes, you are, and it is not helping him."

"Neither is discouraging him and making him feel like the business is more important than him." I sounded completely irrational, even to my own ears and I could see that I hurt his feelings.

"Whatever Faith." My husband's eyes filled with sadness as he put down his book, got up and walked away from me.

That evening, despite our earlier conversation, I fell asleep thanking the Lord for this turn around for Kadin.

I slept better than I had in months, full of hope and peace.

The eight-hour drive to pick up our son from rehab after his sixty-five-day stay seemed even longer this time. Autumn was with us, and we were all excited and a little tense too. Kadin was coming home! We were staying overnight to see his graduation from Redeemer Recovery as a clean and sober young man.

"Autumn! I am going to pop you one!" I only half seriously said looking back at her in the backseat.

"What?" she innocently asked with an ornery grin. "I'm only counting the mile markers, so we know how much further we have to go." She finished, singing "mile marker 118.4." holding the note of the number four for what seemed like a full minute. She had been doing this since we left Maryland.

"Oh, my Lord, Autumn." I laughed as I turned around and gave up for a bit. *I guess she was as excited as we were to see Kadin healthy again.*

"Autumn, that's enough now." Kenny said as sternly as he could muster, smiling at the same time.

She must have known that her dad was getting a little aggravated because she stopped and rolled down the back window and spit something out and SMACK! It came right back in her face. Her look of horror and disgust was priceless.

I busted out laughing and was trying to tell Kenny what happened but was struggling to get it out. Finally, I was able to tell the story and then we were both laughing so hard we had tears running down our faces. My daughter did not see the humor in it though, which made it all the funnier to Kenny and I.

I guess God knew just what we needed to settle us down so that we could make the rest of the trip in peace.

We turned into the long drive down the lane to get to Redeemer, pulled into the lot and parked. We'd arrived. I finished smoking my cigarette and as we got out of the truck, we saw this young man walking toward us. His dark brown hair was cut really close and his face was clean shaven. He was wearing cargo shorts and a plaid button-down shirt. The three of us froze in our tracks.

"Is that Kadin?" one of us asked with wonder. I don't know which of us asked because it was such a surreal moment.

"Hey!" He threw up his big hand with a signature Kadin wave and smiled.

"Oh my goodness, that's Kadin!" I ran toward him, and I could feel the hot tears running down my cheeks.

"You didn't recognize me?" He looked down at me grinning, those big brown eyes sparkling. He hugged me as Autumn and Kenny made their way to us.

"You look wonderful!" Autumn said sincerely as she embraced him.

"Hey Bud, you look good." Kenny gave him a big bear hug.

"Thank you, thank you." He smiled at each one of us.

His skin was glowing. *When did he stop looking healthy?* I wondered for a moment. I gazed up into his beautiful eyes and I saw peace. He didn't just appear good and healthy, I could see he felt it.

The relief that washed over me was like a hot shower on a cold day. I smiled up at him and my spirit felt at ease.

He was allowed to go out with us that night for a bit. We headed back down the long lane and headed to the local diner. As we were eating dinner, I noticed things to which I guess only a mother pays attention. He ordered a child's meal of chicken nuggets with macaroni and cheese and only ate a few bites at that. He didn't eat any dessert, but he did want a Mountain Dew. No caffeine was allowed at Redeemer.

"Did you already eat Kadin?" I asked him.

"No but I'm full, I'm not used to eating a lot here, so I guess I just don't want as much." He shrugged.

I looked at Kenny and he shook his head, silently telling me to *leave it alone.*

We went back to the hotel room for a while, and we laughed and reminisced about funny family memories a bit before it was time for him to go back for the night. We dropped Kadin off at the office building at the entrance of the Redeemer campus sad our evening together had to come to an end.

"I'll see you guys in the morning." He waved good-bye with a smile as he headed inside.

"Wow, he seems really good." The sound of relief in Autumn's voice clearly echoing what we all felt.

"Yeah, he does." Kenny said.

"Yes, he sure does," I agreed wondering if I was the only one who felt like a top wound too tight, afraid to say the wrong thing all evening.

The long drive back down the lane didn't feel so ominous that night. We were all quiet for the fifteen minutes it took us to get back to the hotel. I guess we all had our own thoughts to ponder, but at least today had felt like a celebration.

The next morning, we pulled into the Redeemer compound, the parking lot full of cars and people standing around waiting to attend the "graduation" ceremony at the campus church. We walked up to the large tan brick church and there was Kadin, waiting for us in a sport jacket, dress shirt and tie. I was so proud. *Thank You Lord, our beautiful boy is back.*

He helped us settle into a pew towards the front of the church and proudly introduced us to all the people who were part of his recovery journey up until that point. Counselors and pastors to whom I'd spoken throughout his time there made sure they told us what a great young man Kadin was. My mind kept going back to the school days when the teachers said he was a great kid.

The church was large but unpretentious, able to seat about three hundred people if I had to guess. The musicians began to set up on the platform that spanned the entire front of the church.

As the service started and the music began playing, I watched as my son raised his hands in praise while he sang to the Lord. I don't know if I have ever felt more joy in my life. When he was called up to the stage to give his testimony on his drug abuse and now recovery, he spoke about how his sister nagged him to the point of driving him crazy but he was thankful for her. He thanked Kenny and I and all the people who had been praying and writing him in support. As he ended with giving thanks to God for his recovery, I cried like a baby.

Kadin talked excitedly on the way home about getting back to work, telling us about the jobs he did at Redeemer like putting roofs on the new dorms and learning to cut tiles with a wet saw for the floors, and about the sense of independence and fulfillment he'd felt.

"Wow Kadin, that's huge," Kenny beamed.

I just smiled, holding back tears of pride and joy.

The next couple weeks were fairly quiet, and life went on as usual.

Kadin's birthday came and we had a little cookout at work to celebrate, inviting his grandparents, my mom and pop, like usual. But I noticed something was off with Kadin.

"Hey, you want cake now?" I asked, looking down at him sitting at the table in the warehouse of our party rental building.

"Nah." His head was bent and he didn't make eye contact. Alarms started going off in my head. *Something is wrong. Is he doing drugs? Why won't he look at me? You know why,* my mind answered. *I'm going to throw up.* But I didn't throw up. I didn't talk to Kenny about it either. I denied it to myself, believing whatever "it" was, would go away.

The celebration for Kadin dimmed like a cloud passing over the sun on this beautiful spring day for me. Looking around at everyone laughing and eating, I felt dread creeping in.

Less than two weeks later I couldn't deny it any longer. I answered my phone and heard Kenny's angry voice barking, "I need you to get to the jobsite now Faith!"

CHAPTER SIX

THE LAST TRAIN RIDE

"What is going on Kenny?" I yelled back into the phone as I grabbed my purse and ran out of the office.

"One of the guys called me and told me that Kadin was really high and I needed to come to the job site." He spat back at me.

"No!" I cried. "Where is he now?"

"He better be on the way home, and honestly, I don't even know if he will be able to make it. I was so angry I just told him to get out and go home." Now thanks to your son I can't get the rest of the guys home from this job site because he was our driver!" He was yelling. "This is it! No more chances! He's fired!" The anger in his voice subsided into weariness. "Just get here Faith."

"Oh God, okay, I'm on my way there." I hung up, hot tears stinging my eyes. The drive was a blur of scenery and crowded thoughts. *What are we going to do now? What do I do now?*

The job site was a beautiful event venue, located about five miles away that was having a wedding for the daughter of a family friend. *What a contradiction to my life right now,* I couldn't help jealously thinking.

I don't know how I got there but I managed to pick up the guy who was left at the job site. He was sitting on the curb of the circular entrance of the office at the end of the long winding drive, waiting for me.

I cried and cried as I drove this guy home.

"Why?" I asked…not really to him, but I guess he felt like he needed to answer.

"I don't know why people have to do things like that," the young man answered sadly, shaking his head of shoulder length brown hair, held down only by a black baseball cap with a worn Orioles logo on the front. "It just doesn't make any sense…*he has a good life.*" I glanced over at him and he looked away, then down at his dirty hands in his lap, picking at his fingernails.

We pulled up to his small white stucco home and he got out of my truck and closed the door behind him, "I hope everything works out." He walked up the cracked sidewalk towards the sagging wooden, front porch. I watched as he stepped over a rusted tricycle, discarded and forgotten, that lay on the overgrown grass that hadn't seen a lawnmower in far too long.

"Thanks." I threw up my hand waving goodbye. "See you tomorrow at work."

Oh, how blind I was. I found out a few months later that this guy was Kadin's supplier of the day. Sadly, that same young man died of an overdose just a few years later.

I raced home hoping that Kadin had made it home safely, not thinking that the way I was driving was just as dangerous as my drugged son being on the road.

"Oh, God, oh God." I prayed all the way home. Thank God He knows our hearts and the words don't matter sometimes. I just kept crying out to Him. "Help us Lord!"

I don't think I let out a full breath until I pulled in front of the house to see Kenny's truck in the driveway. Kadin was home. "Thank You Lord." I released my breath like a balloon deflating, not realizing I'd nearly been hyperventilating.

Walking into the house I saw Kenny and Kadin standing at

the top of the steps like a captor and his prisoner. Just standing there. Nobody was saying anything. Kenny's face was almost purple with rage, his six-foot muscular body stiff, his hands clenched by his sides.

I looked over to Kadin to see his head was bent down, his chin almost touching his chest and his body swaying slightly forward and back, his feet not moving. *He can hardly stand up.*

As I climbed the seven steps to reach the top, Autumn suddenly walked in the front door behind me. She was living with her boyfriend in town and attending the local college now but she stopped in to see us every few days. "What's going on?" she asked, seeing me, her father, and her brother, and trying to assess the situation, her eyes going from one of us to another waiting for an answer.

"Kadin's high again!" Kenny shouted at our son, poking his thick forefinger into his chest. "Kadin, I want you out of this house and you are fired! I mean it, get your stuff and get out!" Terror gripped me like I had never felt before I leaped between them like a referee in a boxing ring. *Wait, what? He can't leave like this! We will never see him again!* My mind was screaming.

"I mean it Kadin, get your stuff and GET OUT." Kenny now sounded calm, emphasizing each word in his deep voice. I knew he meant business and would not budge on his demand.

Kadin mumbled something I couldn't understand.

Still, I cried out, "NO!" as I grabbed Kadin's shirt, with both hands, in a death grip. I looked up at this six-foot-four kid knowing that if he left, he was going to die.

"Please, Kadin please," I begged him. I was desperate. Couldn't he see how this was tearing us up?

But as he raised his head up from his chest, I gazed into his face and into those beautiful brown eyes that always sparkled with humor and only saw the dull, hollow look of lifelessness. Looking into those eyes I realized that he was so high he had no idea who I was. He didn't recognize his own mother. *How can I help him if he doesn't even know who I am? How can he not know me?*

"NOW!" Kenny shouted at him.

Kadin reached over to pick up his backpack, barely keeping himself from falling over, and started stumbling down the stairs for the door.

I stood at the top of the steps sobbing as he floundered through the door. Autumn, who'd climbed the stairs by now to comfort me, reached out to me but I pushed her aside and ran down the short hallway into our bedroom and threw myself onto the bed, pounding the mattress and pillows with my fists, like a toddler having a temper tantrum.

How could Kenny be so heartless? Didn't he care about what happened to Kadin? If something happens to Kadin, it will be Kenny's fault and I won't forgive him! My thoughts raced as I prepared for the fight I knew Kenny and I would have when he came in—but I was not ready for his first verbal punch in my gut.

The bedroom door opened and closed quietly.

"Faith," he said sharply but quietly, "you just shoved your daughter away and really hurt her feelings."

"I can't help it!" I wailed at him shocked because he was talking about Autumn and her feelings. *What about me and mine?* "I'm Kadin's mother, what about *my* feelings?" I moaned into the pillow.

"You need to stop this, Faith, this is not helping." He sounded like a father talking to a child.

I sat up on the edge of the bed, wiping my tears. "You think throwing Kadin out to walk the roads and maybe get hit by a car is *helping?*" I spat at him.

"What do you want me to do?" he asked now, sounding more than a little defeated. He sat down on the bed, reached over, turned my chin and made me look at him.

"He will die out there Kenny, he's going to get hurt, I know it!" My head fell onto his chest and I whimpered. "We will lose him forever."

His arms loosely wrapped around me. "I'll go get him, but he's still fired and he's going back to rehab!" He let go and walked out of our room, not giving me a chance to respond.

The loss of his arms around me felt like I had been deserted.

As I walked out of our bedroom a few minutes later, I saw Autumn still standing in the hallway looking dazed. I felt like I was really seeing her for the first time in a long time—her dark jeans and a white Bob Marley T-shirt that said "One Love" on it, her shiny, dark brown hair streaked with caramel-colored highlights, pulled forward around her neck. I saw so many emotions showing on her sweet face and in her sparkling, soft brown eyes—hurt, disappointment, anger, fear, sadness.

"I'm so sorry baby," I said walking to her and wrapping my arms around her. *Lord, how could I hurt this precious girl? I have to get control of myself!*

"It's fine Mom." Her tone of voice made it clear that it really wasn't.

What kind of mother am I? How could I hurt my daughter like that? She'd done nothing wrong, she was only trying to help. I had to help her know how sorry I was, but how? *My God I need help.*

A few minutes later Kenny walked into the house with Kadin following slowly behind. "Just go to your room." Kenny said to him flatly. Without a word Kadin went down to his room in the basement and we heard the door bang shut behind him, the little bell clanging loudly.

Kenny looked at me still standing in the upstairs hallway with Autumn. He walked up the steps shaking his head, then passed me without saying a word. I felt like the kid of a disappointed parent, ashamed of myself. *What do I have to feel bad about?* I thought to myself defiantly, *I'm not the one trying to throw my son out on the street when he needed help.*

"I'll call Redeemer tomorrow and see if we can get him back there." I called after him feeling a little more in control.

"Whatever, Faith." Kenny sounded drained as he walked into our bedroom and closed the door softly behind him.

I looked at Autumn and she was shaking her head too. "You are going to have to stop Mom." She looked at me heartbroken and disappointed.

Now I was starting to feel angry at all of them. "Stop what?" I asked, feeling more than a little insulted. "Stop trying to help my kid from killing himself? Would you want me to stop if it were you?"

"Mom, he has to want it, not you." She sounded so calm and rational. "You can't make him. You can't fix him."

"I have to help him Autumn, you don't understand, he doesn't know what he's doing right now." I groaned. *Why wasn't she understanding? What is wrong with everyone? Am I the only one who cares about Kadin?* My mind was whirling with questions that had no answers.

Sleep that night was impossible. Neither Kenny nor I could settle ourselves enough to rest. I kept listening for any sound that could possibly indicate Kadin might be trying to sneak out.

Morning finally came and the man who answered the phone at Redeemer Recovery told me that Kadin would have to fill out the application and go through the whole process again. I was frantic. "Please help us," I begged him, "we need to get him back there right away."

He was sympathetic but firm. "Mrs. Addair," he said calmly, "we will do the best we can to get him through the process."

As I hung up the phone, I felt the bile rise up in my throat. *I'm going to be sick*, I thought. I could feel my body trembling and my mind was screaming, *HURRY!*

"Come on Kadin!" I yelled downstairs. "It's time to go."

"Yeah, I'm coming." He yelled back up.

"Okay so you have everything?" I asked for probably the hundredth time.

"Yeah," he said drowsily.

"Okay so this train will take you to Washington, DC and then you will get on the train that will take you to North Carolina." I reminded him. "Don't forget that you have to get on the train to Charlotte. It will be about ten hours so make sure you get close to the bathroom." I added the last part with a chuckle, trying to lighten the mood.

"I know Mom, you wrote all the directions down." He showed me the paper with the instructions I'd written down.

"I know, I'm just reminding you. But when you get to Charlotte you have to call right away because you only have a twenty-five-minute window to find the shuttle bus that will take you to Redeemer."

"Okay Mom." He sighed with exasperation.

It was time to go to the train station. It was just he and I this time. I looked over at him as I drove down Pulaski Highway towards Aberdeen. Already I could tell he was high. *Oh God*, I thought, *how is he going to make it down there? What if he cuts out and runs and doesn't even go?*

The twenty-minute wait for the train dragged on for what seemed like hours. Finally, we heard and felt the rumbling of the train from a distance. With a short horn blast, it pulled into the station. The shrill sound of the brakes echoed the relieved breath coming from my lungs.

I felt like I was going to be sick again. I watched as my baby got on the train and I was so scared, tired, relieved. What kind of mother is relieved that her child is leaving her? *I can't help him, so I'm happy he's leaving? What is wrong with me? Lord, how do I help him?*

He waved at me before stepping onto the train, calling over his shoulder, "I love you, Mom!"

"I love you Kadin." His name caught in my throat.

With the screech of the rails and the hiss of the brakes releasing on the train, he was on his way.

Gone, again.

I don't remember the walk back to my truck but somehow, I made it. I sat in the parking lot of the train station sobbing and sweating. Why would I expect this time to be any different? I cried to myself. I don't have the answers and I don't know how to help him. *Why won't You help him, Lord?*

The longer I sat there sobbing, the angrier I was getting with myself and the part I played in him being high this time.

I went over the conversations we had a few days before. Could I have done anything different? Should I have done anything different?

Memories sprang to the surface of my mind…

"Mom," Kadin had said with his voice shaking as he sat down across from me on the back porch. "I'm not going to make it, I can't." His eyes pleaded with me as his hands clenched and unclenched turning from white to red, again and again, his leg bouncing from his knee down to his foot in jerky movements that showed he was a wreck.

"Baby, you only have three more days, you're going to be okay, I promise," I said with more surety than I felt. "Go lay down for a while and it will help the time go by."

"Yeah, okay." He'd walked back into the house slowly, his head down, shoulders slumped. Somehow his six foot-four body looked so much smaller as he walked away.

As I sat there on the back porch praying, the hot tears had run down my face plopping onto the pages of the book I'd been trying to read for over an hour.

"God, help him." I cried aloud.

The next evening on the way home from work, he'd asked me to run him to the store to get cigarettes. He asked to go to a specific store, and I took him. I knew that he was going to get more than his cigarettes. God help me I knew it and I took him anyway! All day long he had been as anxious as a lion in a cage, and I was just waiting for him to escape.

What kind of mother am I? What kind of person does this? I'd railed at myself as I waited in the parking lot of the liquor shop. Then I'd reasoned with myself, trying to maintain my sanity. *He's leaving in two more days and then he will be okay. At least he won't sneak out of the house and I'll know where he'll be.* My mind was trying to rationalize why I was sitting out here waiting while my son was inside buying this K2 or Spice or whatever people called it.

This isn't that serious anyway, it's not like it's heroin, I thought to myself, trying to make myself feel a little less responsible for helping him do what he was doing.

Maybe he isn't buying it, maybe he is just buying cigarettes. But I knew the truth.

He got back in the truck and we headed home. I didn't ask him because I really didn't want to hear him say it out loud. I didn't need him to. I could see it all over his body. He was more at ease and talkative. He had what he needed—he had his drugs.

I wish I could say I would do things differently. I would like to say that even knowing that he was going to get this garbage that was poison to his lungs, I wouldn't have taken him to the store. I would like to say that, but I can't. I don't know if I would do things differently, but I like to think that I would. I would like to think that I would have faith and trust in God for Kadin and tell him "no." I'd like to think that.

So, I had to wait and wallow in my guilt while he journeyed back to rehab. Every minute that ticked by on the clock in my office was a reminder that, tick—you took him to the store, tock—you know he was going to buy drugs, tick—he will get off the train, tock—and get more serious drugs, tick—he won't make it to rehab, tock—it's all my fault.

The ding of my phone at nine-forty-five that night was from Kadin texting:

"Phew, made it on the shuttle bus headed to Redeemer so not too far now." He ended his text with, *"Mom, I love you more than you will ever know, and I hope you will forgive me again for all I've put you and Dad through."*

"Of course, we forgive you Kadin, we love you!" I texted back to him.

The question was, could I forgive myself?

CHAPTER SEVEN

HOMECOMING

Thirty days went by fast this time. Kadin was more positive and upbeat during our phone conversations during this second rehab stay.

I surprised him by flying him home because he had never been on an airplane, and I thought that would be exciting for him.

We saw him coming towards us from the baggage claim area with that big hand raised up in the air. "Hey!" he yelled.

"Kadin, you look great," I said to him, and he really did. He wore a clean dress shirt and khakis, his light brown eyes were bright, his dark brown hair was cut short and neatly combed, and he was smiling. Our son was back.

"You look good, Bud." Kenny said to Kadin, hugging him.

"How did you like flying?" I asked him.

"It was cool!" He said enthusiastically. "I was a little nervous for a minute, but it was cool."

"I thought you would like it." I smiled.

As we headed out of the airport and walked to our truck, I noticed that Kadin was already texting on his phone. I wanted to know who it was, but I thought I would wait to ask him until he had time to settle. He wasn't allowed to have his phone in rehab, so I thought it was odd that he was already on it.

About a week after he got home, Kadin started hanging out with a girl who didn't live far from us.

I followed him into the kitchen one night as he was pouring some milk into a glass and I asked him. "Who is this girl?" I paced nervously, trying unsuccessfully to look nonchalant.

He closed the refrigerator door and turned to look at me, leaning against the sink.

"She wrote to me at Redeemer, she goes to Phil's church. Her name is Hannah.

"Ah, so she lives nearby? Well, we'd like to meet her sometime."

"It's not really like that Mom."

I wasn't sure exactly what he meant by that, but I played along. "Okay well I just want you to know that we are interested in how life is going for you."

"Yeah, okay mom." He chuckled and rolled his eyes, walked out of the kitchen and down to his room.

I figured this was probably something just to fill in his time, so I didn't want to make a big deal out of it. He seemed happy and healthy and came to work every day, so I felt like everything was good. *I should just back off,* I thought.

But over the next few weeks the relationship seemed to start getting serious quickly and I worried. I'm not sure about what exactly—I just felt like something was wrong. Maybe it was mother's intuition or loss of control, I wasn't sure which, probably both.

Redeemer Recovery was having their annual homecoming weekend in October and I thought it would be great for Kadin to go so he could celebrate his recovery with the others who had made it. I would like to say that was my only reason for trying to talk him into going, but I know I was also secretly hoping that Kadin would go, and at the same time distance himself from Hannah and get a clearer picture of where his life was headed.

It wasn't because I didn't like her, I just thought their relationship was moving way too quickly and her family was rushing it along.

Hannah was in her last year of High School so she invited Kadin to go to her Senior Homecoming dance. Kadin was dressed in black slacks and a white shirt, his aqua tie matching the color of her short, off-the-shoulder dress. Hannah's long brunette hair was pulled back from her small oval-shaped face, her curls flowing down to her tiny waist. As she leaned back against Kadin for a photo, I had a flash of apprehension, about what I still don't know.

While I was pushing Kadin to go to Redeemer's Homecoming, Kenny wasn't as gung-ho about it. Of course, it would mean our son would have to spend a weekend away from work and it was the last busy weekend of the year for our events business. At least that was the way I interpreted my husband's reaction.

One evening, a few weeks before the Homecoming weekend, we sat in the living room eating dinner on snack trays in front of the television.

"I don't know Faith," Kenny looked down at his meatloaf, "I don't think it's a good idea."

"Why?" I asked him huffily, spearing a bite with my fork and shoving it into my mouth.

"I just don't have a good feeling about it. But it's up to him I guess." He looked at the television and I knew the conversation was over.

He probably just doesn't want to lose the help, I thought, turning my attention back to the mindless comedy show on TV, my mind made up that Kadin should go.

The next day at work Kadin walked into the office, "Hey Kadin have you thought about Homecoming?"

"I don't know if I want to go Mom." He looked down at

the paperwork in his hands.

"I think it might be good for you." I coaxed.

"Maybe, I'll think about it." He walked out of the office and back into the warehouse.

"Okay, good." I called after him, "let me know."

As usual, I was sticking my nose in, pushing and preparing to make things easy for him. I was just trying to help…that was my job after all.

I knocked on Kadin's bedroom door a few nights later, and when there was no answer, I opened it, peering inside. Kadin was lying on his bed, texting on his phone, which seemed to be glued to his hands all the time lately.

"Hey, I checked and I can get you a hotel room for about two-hundred bucks for the weekend so you won't have to rush around and you'll be able to attend all the events that Redeemer has planned." I tried to hold the anxiety in my tone at bay.

Kadin didn't look up from his phone, so I continued. "Just let me know if you want me to reserve the room."

"Okay Mom, go ahead and get the hotel, I'll go." He sounded resigned, not thrilled at all about it.

"I don't want you to go if you don't want to Kadin," I lied to him and to myself. I just wanted him to be excited about it because I was.

"I'll go Mom, okay?" I took the cue that he was done talking and quietly closed the bedroom door behind me, not feeling like I'd won at all, my victory temporarily tinged with guilt that I had made this happen by force. Why didn't he get it that I was trying to encourage him to do something good for himself?

A couple weeks later, Kadin was getting ready to leave for the Homecoming weekend.

"Okay so you have the jack in your car and the directions just in case?" Kenny asked Kadin as we went out to his little black Saturn car, to send him off to the reunion that October morning.

"Yeah, Mom printed them for me, but I have my GPS on my phone." He wiggled his phone in the air for us to see and smirked.

Kenny rolled his eyes, "You can't always depend on that son," he said. "If you don't have service, what are you gonna do?" This was an ongoing friendly argument with Kenny and the guys at work because they all relied on GPS, while Kenny and Eric, his partner, were old school. "None of these kids today can read a dang map!" my husband would always say.

"I packed you a bunch of snacks and stuff, so you have something to eat on the way down, just be careful." *What was I thinking?* I asked myself, suddenly wanting to talk him out of going. I was sending my nineteen-year-old baby on an eight-hour road trip all by himself. But it was too late now.

"I love you." I said instead, hoping and praying for the best. "Have fun, okay?"

"Okay Mom, love you guys." He got into his car to head out.

"Text me when you get there, please!" I yelled as he was backing down the driveway.

"Okay!" He yelled back and his music began to blare. We could hear him as he drove off down the road and left the neighborhood.

As I watched him drive away, I thought to myself, this should help him recharge his batteries, build himself back up and see how good he is doing, right?

I was so wrong.

Kadin texted that night that he had arrived safely. That was the last time I heard from him that weekend.

He arrived back in Maryland on Sunday evening but didn't come home.

We heard from Hannah that night.

"Hi Miss Faith," she said over the phone. "I'm at the hospital with Kadin."

"Why?" I asked nervously, my whole body shaking. "What's wrong?" My mind started playing out all the worst scenarios.

"He fell down the steps last night while he was there at Redeemer, and he has a really bad headache and he's throwing up." Hannah sounded worried. "So, my mom and I brought him here, they said he probably has a concussion."

"How in the world did that happen?" I asked her as I paced the kitchen.

"He said he was goofing off heading out of the hotel and just fell down the steps." She didn't sound too convincing, but I tried hard to believe her. "I'll call you if anything changes, we'll just take him home with us."

"Okay, tell him we love him and hope he feels better." I said helplessly. "Talk to you tomorrow, thanks for calling." I hung up, my heart filled with dread. *Lord, I hope they don't mess up and give him pain medicine.*

For the next two weeks we didn't see a whole lot of Kadin. It was a slow time at work, so he spent most of his time with Hannah at her house.

When I did see him, I noticed he was avoiding making eye contact and just didn't want to talk, and alarms started going off in my head—the same sirens that used to go off when he was younger, but I attempted to ignore back then. I couldn't ignore them now. So, every chance I got, I would begin my interrogation.

"You doing okay Bud?" I'd ask.

"I'm tired Mom, I'm going to go to bed. Love you." He would answer.

"Staying clean?" I would ask him only half-jokingly.

"Yes! Geez Mom, you need to stop smothering me." He would say. Yeah right, I'd think to myself, like that will ever happen.

"How many days clean today?" I asked him one afternoon.

"I'm not really sure." He almost stuttered as he walked away from me.

Was I paranoid or was it weird that he didn't know how many days he'd been clean? I thought everyone knew how many days they had.

Exactly one month after his hospital stay on the night of November 28, 2013, Kadin came into the house and started to walk directly towards the bathroom. As he passed me, I called his name.

"Kadin?"

"I got to go to the bathroom," he murmured without looking at me, and closed the door behind him.

I waited for him to finish and when he opened the door, I glared at him. The jig was up.

"Kadin, I want you to take a drug test." I said to him.

"What?" he asked sharply..

"You heard me, I want you to take a drug test." I repeated.

He stood there, his shoulders slowly falling. "No." His voice just a whisper.

"No?" I asked. "You are not willing to take a drug test?"

"No, I'm not." He didn't look at me.

"Why not, Kadin?" I asked stupidly, knowing the answer.

He didn't answer me, he just stood there, his shoulders drooping, his head facing down as if he was looking for answers on the hardwood floor below.

"What's going on?" Kenny asked as he walked in the house and saw our son just standing there outside the bathroom door.

"Kadin won't take a drug test." I said matter-of-factly as if he should have known this.

"Does he need to?" he asked me. Then he looked over at Kadin. Kenny's face was a stone mask. "Kadin, we need you to take a drug test," he told our son calmly.

I looked at him and wondered how on earth he could be so calm. Was I the only one here panicking right now? *God, here we go again.*

"I can't Dad." Kadin said.

"Why not?" Kenny's voice rose an octave, his face turning red with anger now.

"I won't pass it." Kadin said quietly.

He proceeded to tell us the whole story as Kenny and I sat

in the living room listening.

It all began when he went to Redeemer Homecoming and a few of the very people who were there supposedly "celebrating" were not doing so in the way we believed. Kadin told us they were partying at the hotel and he was so high that he woke up on the cement stairs outside the hotel in a blackout, his head aching. He didn't attend Homecoming at Redeemer at all.

As we talked that evening, I knew that I had lost all control. I felt my body trembling like I had been out in the freezing cold. How had this happened? I tried to stuff down the guilt I felt over encouraging my son to go in the first place so I wouldn't throw up. *What do we do next?*

"Well, what do you want to do Kadin?" Kenny finally asked after a few dreadful moments of silence.

I looked at my husband, baffled and alarmed at his lunacy. *Why are you asking Kadin what he wants to do?* I wanted to scream at him. *He doesn't know what to do!*

"Well, I don't want to go back to Redeemer." Kadin nervously picked at a loose thread on the arm of the upholstered chair where he sat, looking down at his lap.

Kenny and I both looked at each other and nodded, quietly agreeing that it wasn't where he should go this time.

We knew Redeemer was an amazing rehab facility. They had terrific administrators, counselors, and minsters who did great work, and we vowed to continue to support them and would highly recommend them to anyone who truly wanted help recovering from addiction.

But we knew at that point that it was going to take much longer than thirty days…and a change of scenery, for Kadin to have a chance at recovery.

CHAPTER EIGHT

THIRD TIME'S THE CHARM?

Here we go again, I thought. We (meaning I) were filling out more paperwork and getting the medical tests done again but this time it was for a whole year in rehab.

Kadin was not happy.

As he sat by my desk in my office, he did nothing but complain.

"I don't want to go for a year, it's ridiculous. A year? That's crazy."

"Kadin, do you want to get clean?" I kept calm, trying to keep any emotion or inflection out of my voice. I was done with all this drama. I had some boundaries now. I put my hands on my hips and leaned towards him.

"Yes!" he answered adamantly.

"Okay well then this is what you are going to have to do. We've tried the shorter rehab stays and they haven't worked."

He grumbled and complained but we continued with the process.

It was about a week before it would be time to take Kadin down to Virginia for a new rehab stint, he came upstairs and began talking to Kenny and me as we sat in the living room. As we'd gotten closer to the time for him to leave, he'd become more agitated with each passing day.

"I really don't want to go for a year, I don't need to." Kadin's voice was laced with desperation. "I haven't used anything for almost a month already." He paced from the living room to the kitchen and back then stopped to glare at us as if to make us understand how serious he was.

"Kadin, this is your choice." Kenny sat forward in his recliner and faced Kadin, equally calm. "You can either commit to doing this one-year rehab or you can leave our house. You cannot live here if you are using drugs."

Our son's blank stare made it look like a glass of ice water had been thrown at him.

This time I was on Kenny's side. "Kadin," I said in my most pacifying voice, "We love you, but we can't help you kill yourself. You are nineteen years old, and you have to get yourself together. Is this how you want to live for the rest of your life?"

The drive to the rehab facility called Renewal Recovery in Virginia was much shorter than the one to Redeemer, only a little over four hours. True to his word, Kadin hadn't used any drugs for about a month and he was feeling okay, but Kenny and I still believed he needed much more time clean and sober before he really would *be* okay.

We could tell that Kadin was nervous and by the time we arrived, Kenny and I were too.

Two twenty-something-year-old men were sitting at a long, paper-strewn desk in the small office that was darkly paneled, dimly lit and messy.

They had their backs to us and didn't seem to care that anyone had come into the office.

"Hi, we are here to check our son in," I said to their backs.

"Who are you?" one of the guys asked sharply, turning to look at each of us slowly as if we had interrupted them. His dark hoodie, I couldn't tell the actual color because the office was so dark, was shredded around the wrists and his jeans looked at least two sizes too big for him. I thought he looked like a bum and acted like one too. He was not welcoming, to say the least.

"This is Kadin Addair, and we are his parents, Kenny and Faith. As I made the introduction, the young man continued to stare at us blankly, his head and forehead shrouded by his hoodie.

Then it dawned on me. They had no idea who we were or why we were there.

"You didn't know he was coming?" My voice sounded shrill in my own ears and I started to feel my old 'friend' fear sneak up. *What kind of place was this?*

"Nope, you have to come back some other time," the other guy said rudely without even turning to look at us. "There is nobody to do intake on the weekends. Call on Monday."

"No, I don't think so," I said, a little snarky now. "We were told to be here today and here we are."

"I'm sorry, what did you say your name was?" A very tall gentleman who appeared to be about thirty years old walked in from another room towards us. He was neatly dressed in a sports shirt and slacks, and his welcoming smile helped deescalate my increasing frustration.

"Kadin Addair," our son answered.

"We filled out all the paperwork and Pastor Phil Meekins called and spoke with someone in your office several times about Kadin," I stated with a little more sass than was probably necessary. Clearly all my attitude had not vanished yet.

Here I go again, trying to take control.

"Pastor Phil, yes he is a great guy." The gentleman said. "No, it's all okay just let me get things together and we will get him settled in. My name is Michael, and I am the interim manager for Renewal for Youth." Michael gave us a gesture of welcome and talked to Kadin in a warm voice.

"Kadin, you can leave your bags here and I will show you all around the campus." He led the three of us out of the office. Michael gave us a tour of the campus, showing us the dining area, the dorm rooms and the rec room which had ping pong and pool tables. At each new building, his pride became more evident. He loved this place. It was a beautiful campus with several dogs wandering around too. That would be good for Kadin, I thought.

As he was giving us the tour, Michael told us his testimony of how he ended up at Renewal.

"I was into all kinds of bad things and one night I ended up with eight bullets in me, one which is still there. I finally ended up here at Renewal Recovery and that is when God got hold of me and helped me to get a hold of my life. Now I am speaking all over the world, sharing my testimony and sharing what God did and is still doing for me." You could hear the awe and wonder in his voice.

"That is amazing," I said, and it was.

"Yes, that's why I'm moving on from here in about a week or so. Those two guys that you met in the office earlier will be in charge while I'm gone until someone else is brought in to be the new director of Renewal," he finished.

"Wow, where are you going?" I asked, feeling a little uneasy but thinking that mostly it was because I was getting ready to leave Kadin again.

"I'm heading to the Dominican Republic and Ghana," he answered with excitement.

We finished the tour and before we left, Michael spoke with Kenny and I briefly to reassure us.

"Believe me, this place will be the best place for him. It made all the difference in me—it changed my life. I can guarantee that if I hadn't been court-ordered at the time to come here, I would not be alive today."

As we left and headed towards home, I felt absolute dread creeping up on me. I felt like I had just left Kadin in the lion's den. The only guy I trusted, Michael the director, was leaving in a week and those two rude young men would be in charge.

Less than a week later, Kadin called us at ten-thirty at night.

"Mom, you need to come get me," he demanded. I had just begun to doze off after attempting to read the first page of a new book for the umpteenth time on the living room couch.

"What? Kadin, no we are not coming to get you. Just hang in there," I said to him, feeling my heartbeat jumping in my chest once again.

"I already left," he stated flatly.

"What?!" I sat up, the book flying off my lap onto the floor. "What do you mean you left?"

Kenny was in the kitchen getting a snack and a glass of milk, rushed in to stand next to me, putting his hand on my shoulder.

"You have to tell him either he stays there, or he can't come home," Kenny said in a frenzied whisper.

"I had them drive me to the bus stop so I could go home." Kadin replied.

"Kadin, this is ridiculous, you have to go back there right now," I pleaded. "You have to stick to this."

"Seriously Mom, these guys are doing drugs in our rooms right in front of me. I would be better off at home."

"Kadin, come on now," I said to him, doubting what he was saying.

"Mom, right now I'm really cold, it's raining, and I'm starving." He sounded miserable and my mom's heart was tearing apart. We were still having nasty winter weather on the East Coast in early March.

Saying what I said next to my son was probably the hardest thing I ever had to do. "Kadin, Dad and I love you, but you better call Renewal and ask them to come get you because you can't come home." I mustered all of the firmness I could into my voice.

As I hung up the phone I leaned on Kenny's chest and cried. His strong arms comforted me, but I felt like my insides were ripping apart. *What kind of mother tells her child that he can't come home?*

Over the following few weeks Kadin's voice and attitude sounded completely different. There seemed to be a seriousness but also a positivity in him that hadn't been there before. Yet, while our son's resolve seemed to improve, Kenny and I got more and more worried. With nowhere to go, Kadin had gone back to Renewal and we would talk to him once a week. But every time I tried to get through to the office of Renewal and ask for the director, I got the same response. If someone answered the phone at all he'd say something like, "No ma'am, no director, just me doing all the work." Whoever answered would also never be willing to give me his name.

The more we spoke with Kadin the more alarmed we became. Kadin told us at the nearby car wash where most of the residents worked, they were either doing drugs or selling them there. When I spoke with Kadin, usually at the car wash because I could never get an answer at Renewal, he told us this was the norm there.

"The guys are getting high in our rooms and there is nobody here to drug test us so they are getting away with it," he would tell us. "It's crazy."

After almost two months of the same things going on and still no director in place, Kenny and I prayed about it and talked with Autumn. I needed to make sure that it wasn't me being… well…me…and trying to take control of the situation.

We all ended up in agreement that something sketchy was going on at this rehab, and we needed to get Kadin out of there.

My husband and I spoke with Kadin over the phone that day and laid out what we expected from him and what we would do to support him if he came home.

As we talked about the situation he was in now, Kadin said, "I'm going to be surrounded by this everywhere, so I have to get used to it, but I know that I can't ever do drugs again. It isn't a matter of wanting or not wanting to, I realize that I cannot do them because I'll die."

"Kadin," Kenny said, "If we bring you home, we need you to agree with your mom and I that for one year you will be accountable to us. That means that you agree to take random drug tests whenever we want to give them to you."

"Okay, yes I will, no problem."

"And you agree not to use your car for the first six months." Kenny continued.

"Okay." He answered back into the phone.

"Okay then," Kenny responded. "Let them know we are coming to get you and we will see you on Thursday."

Autumn rode down with us to pick him up and the moment we saw him we were all relieved. He looked healthy and happy.

We knew the next phase of recovery was going to be especially tough with our son living at home, but it finally felt like we were headed in the right direction.

∞

About six months after he came home to live with us, Kadin decided he wanted to visit one of the recovery houses in our hometown in Maryland.

"Kadin, you have to be careful." Kenny told him. "Sometimes it's not a good idea to see people you used to hang around."

"I agree Kadin." I nodded.

"It's okay guys," he said. "I'm not worried about that. I'm just going to see how some of my old buddies are doing and stuff."

It wasn't too long after that when Kadin began to go to Narcotics Anonymous meetings. I believe they made a big difference and helped him.

That is also where he met his future wife, Aria.

Kenny and I agreed that at some point our son was going to have to start making his own decisions—he was twenty years old at this point. We needed to step back and let him. *But how?*

Kadin seemed to be doing okay in his recovery.
Now I felt like it was time to look at my own.

CHAPTER NINE

IT TAKES A VILLAGE

I'll never forget the day I had to tell my mom that her grandson was a drug addict. It broke my heart. She loved Kadin so much and I knew that she would worry herself sick about him.

"Mom, Kadin is addicted to heroin." I choked out as scalding tears poured down my face.

"Oh no!" she cried, and her hands flew to her mouth. As she reached out to hug me her anguished sobs racked her slender body.

"How did this happen?" she asked, her mascara dripping down from the lashes of her beautiful bright green eyes. Her voice filled with barely controlled emotion.

"I don't know Mom, I really don't." I smoothed back her golden-brown hair framing her thin face.

We sat out in the warehouse outside my office that December morning for what seemed like hours, surrounded by thousands of chairs, hundreds of tables, tents and dance floor pieces all stacked, around the perimeter of the huge warehouse, all waiting and ready to be delivered for the next round of parties. It was as dark and dreary outside as I'm sure we both felt inside. We were frozen in this moment of torment and partying was the last thing on our minds.

We cried for a long time as Mom went through a list of a few people she wasn't going to tell. "They love him so much that this will just break their hearts and scare them to death. I don't want them thinking that Kadin is a bad boy because he isn't." She burst out crying again.

Oh boy did I understand that. I learned very quickly to surround myself with people I felt I could trust. The last thing I needed was to feel like Kadin was being judged or worse yet, like I was. It is always surprising how many people will tell you how they would do things differently without ever walking in your shoes.

Along with Kenny, Autumn, and I, we had my mom and pop, along with Kenny's parents, and we were blessed with the numerous dear friends that God placed into our lives.

Eric and Alicia were two of those friends. They came into our lives many years before we had our kids and I believe, as always, God knew what He was doing when He put us together. A couple our age with a good marriage and values that paralleled ours, Eric and Alicia grew to be our best friends and then Kenny and Eric became business partners in their party rental company almost twenty years ago. They'd become like family.

They felt our devastation and fear. Very early on in Kadin's addiction, Alicia and I made a promise that at nine p.m. every night she would pray, in tandem with me, for Kadin and his recovery—and she did, right along with me, through it all.

On one of those days after a phone call from Kadin telling me he was really struggling, I asked Kenny and Eric to come into our work office. I told Eric and Alicia that he needed extra prayer. Alicia's dark brown eyes filled with concern as her long dark lashes beaded with tears. Bowing his head, Eric's black beard streaked with gray touched his chest, all four of us held hands and began to pray for him together.

As we continued through this journey, the amount of support and prayers we received was amazing.

What I didn't know was that every time I sent out a prayer request text to about fifty families on our prayer chain, one of these people would turn out to be a great supporter for me.

He was a young man named David whose family members were friends with us. I thought it was very kind that he was so supportive of Kadin.

One day I reminded David what an encouragement he'd been to me. He and Mary, his pretty young wife, had brought me a computer that I had bought from them. As they sat in their car in my driveway that sunny and warm early evening in summer, we talked through the open driver window.

"David, I just want to again tell you again how much I appreciate how encouraging you were to me during Kadin's time in rehab."

"Faith," he looked up at me from his car window, "you don't know how much you encouraged me." I must have given him a puzzled look, so he went on to explain. "I thought you knew that I struggled with addiction too."

"What?" This took my breath away. I had no idea. "When David? How did we not know this?" Now the fear for this young man was creeping into my heart and I knew that I was going to have to hit my knees for him as well.

"Remember when I had the four-wheeler accident?"

"Yes, I do, you scared us all to death." I answered with a chuckle knowing that he was well now.

"Well, that is when I got addicted to Oxycontin. It happened so fast but I'm good now." He looked over at Mary and squeezed her hand. They were an adorable couple—she with her blonde hair and green eyes a sharp contrast to his dark hair and dark eyes. It was hard to imagine this fine young man had been a drug addict. But, then again, it wasn't so hard to imagine because our own "fine young man" was a drug addict.

"Thank God!" I breathed a sigh. "Now if you do anything

like that again I'm gonna smack the daylights out of you," I finished lightheartedly.

"I won't," he said, "believe me, I won't." He got out of the car and raised up to his well over six-foot height and bent over to give me a hug.

Yet again God amazed me and proved that there are no coincidences in the situations or circumstances that He allows us to go through. I praised God for David's recovery.

As my eyes were opening, I began to see those around me who were clearly suffering with addiction and started to realize some things about myself. I was not helping my kid.

God, that just made me sick thinking about it, but it was the truth. I finally came to the realization that our son could only help himself, and as long as I was in the way, he would never be able to do that. If I kept going the way I was going, I would love him to his death.

This did not sound right to me at first when this truth was first introduced by a friend of mine named Lisa, whose daughter had been an addict for fifteen years. Lisa had not heard from her daughter in almost six years and yet, this mother seemed to be okay, happy even.

"How do you hold on to your sanity?" I asked her one day as we were having Bible Study at her friend Michele's house.

"I had to stop trying to do it for her." She told me, her hazel eyes locked on mine.

"Yes, but how do you know that's the right thing to do?" I challenged her, wary at first. *I love Kadin and what if he needs my help?* I questioned silently, not wanting to imply Lisa didn't love her own daughter.

"Oh, I didn't know, but God did," she answered simply as we walked down the driveway to our vehicles. "Go back to what you know of God and start there, He will do the rest."

So that's what I did. I started looking for answers in the Bible, searching out scriptures that reminded me that God was in control.

I found the passage in Matthew 6:25-26 where Jesus spoke and said, *"Therefore I say to you, do not worry about your life, what you will eat or what you will drink; nor about your body, what you will put on. Is not life more than food and the body more than clothing? Look at*
the birds of the air, for they neither sow nor reap nor gather into barns; yet your heavenly Father feeds them. Are you not of more value than they?"

I wasn't worried about what I was needing to eat, drink or wear but I *was* worried all the time and I knew that this applied to what I was feeling because then, in verses 33-34, Jesus continued. *"But seek first the kingdom of God and His righteousness, and all these things shall be added to you. Therefore, do not worry about tomorrow, for tomorrow will worry about its own things. Sufficient for the day is its own trouble."*

Simply put, I was not trusting God. How could that be? I loved God. I had faith. But if I did, why was my worrying eating me alive and making me an unpleasant person to be around? Wow! It was like a God spanking.

At any given time after that, you would hear me chanting Psalm 46:1. *"God is our refuge and strength, a very present help in trouble,"* and Psalm 62:7, *"In God is my salvation and my glory; the rock of my strength, and my refuge, is in God."*

So, I would take the dogs outside during the early afternoon at work, sometimes right after I ate lunch, and as they did their business, I would get down to His.

One of those days when I was working and although it was only nine-o'-clock in the morning, I knew that if I didn't get out there with Him, I was going to lose my peace. As I started doing my walking laps around our parking lot and was struggling with how to pray, I began to feel the hot tears warming my cheeks as they flowed from my eyes…and then the words came tumbling out…

"Father, I thank you for all that you bless us with. Lord, my salvation is my greatest gift. I am so grateful for Your mercy and grace, and I know that I can come to You with my heart you love him more than we do Father, so we trust You and ask that Your will be done. Lord, I ask that you help me to remember that this is not my battle to fight but his and Yours. I pray this in Your Son's name, amen."

After my prayer that day I realized I was praying pretty loud and some of the workers at the building next to ours probably heard me crying out to God and I just smiled to myself as I gathered the pups and took them back into the office to finish the day of work. I was no longer ashamed or worried what others thought of me.

I also began to see Kenny as God would have me see him— a strong and loving man who is faithful and dependable. I could trust him, and trust was not something I was able to give easily in the past. But God showed me all the love and support and encouragement that Kenny had shown, not just to me but to Kadin. My selfish and controlling heart and mind just wasn't seeing the truth because it wasn't the truth according to *my* plans.

God helped me to see what Kenny had been showing me for the last thirty years…we were on the same team, and that team was our marriage. Kenny supported my brokenness throughout our years together simply by loving me. I began to see that Kenny wasn't being mean to Kadin, but instead he loved him so much that he wanted our son to be the best he could be—and that was not going to happen by allowing him to continue to destroy his body by enabling him.

Oh, make no mistake, Kenny spent many sleepless nights worrying and praying for Kadin—but he saw the man that he was *supposed* to be, while I was still trying to raise and control a little boy. Kadin was no longer a little boy of course, but because I wanted to control everything, that is exactly how I was treating him. God revealed to me how strong Kenny was forced to be because he was battling his fear for Kadin while battling me to stay on his team.

I looked forward to Sundays at our small church, the North East Church of God. When I walked up those concrete steps and through the front door into the vestibule, I immediately felt comforted. Looking at those oak pews filled with God's faithful children ready to worship Him was like walking into His loving arms.

Those precious parishioners greeted us, eagerly waiting to hear how Kadin was doing, then they would praise God if he was doing well—and hit their knees with us at the altar when he wasn't.

One afternoon at work as I was remembering back to the day we took Autumn to college and recalling how panicked and anxious I felt that day, God showed me a scripture. Now I don't mean He opened my bible and said, "here it is Faith, read this." I'm sure He felt like He needed to do just that sometimes, to get through to me. But I believe wholeheartedly that a Facebook post and the bookmark found in an old book both showed me what I needed, and that was from Him. It was the verse Isaiah 26:3— *"You will keep him in perfect peace, whose mind is stayed on You, because he trusts in You."*

Okay, simple, I told myself. I needed to keep my mind on God and trust Him and He would keep me in perfect peace. *Whoa! Simple and profound at the same time.* This is still my go to scripture because I am not willing to lose my peace. But notice how it doesn't say that He will make sure that everything goes the way I want it. I didn't notice that at first…yeah, it took me just a little longer to get that.

But finally, after years of failing to turn my son over to God's care, now I knew that if I kept helping Kadin the way I was, I would help him kill himself. I knew now I could best help Kadin by not helping him anymore. For so long, I wanted God to do it my way because I thought my way was the right way and I wanted Him to fix Kadin here and now…but it all had nothing to do with me. I finally discovered this was not about me at all.

It was the night our church volunteered to feed the homeless and hungry people of Elkton. The group at Mariners Park that January evening was large, cold and hungry, and they wanted to hurry up and get their food and go back to their tents for the night. The sun was just lowering itself below the tree line and the chill of the evening air made our breaths puff out in a cloud of steam.

I walked toward a young woman, maybe in her late twenties or early thirties, sitting on a picnic table bench. She was a new face to this group of homeless people in the community that our church would help feed once a month.

"Hi, how are you doing tonight?" I gingerly sat down a couple feet away from her on the bench.

She shrugged her shoulders which were covered with many layers of clothing that were caked with dried-up mud.

"What's your name?" I moved closer to her.

"Cara." She answered barely above a whisper.

"Hi Cara, my name is Faith. Can I pray with you today?" I looked down at her and she nodded without looking up. I could tell she had once been beautiful. But now she appeared malnourished, gaunt, her brown hair stringy, her cheeks sallow. After praying with her, I scooted closer to her and talked to her for a short time.

"Are you from around here?"

She nodded, her eyes downcast, but didn't say a word.

"How did your life go in this direction? What happened?"

At first, I could see that she didn't want to talk. Maybe she was too ashamed.

"Cara, if you don't want to answer me that is absolutely fine, I'm not judging you, believe me. We can just sit here and talk about anything you want to talk about."

She looked up at me and at that moment, I felt fear grip me and I wanted to wrap my arms around her and never let go. The look of complete despair in her dark hollow eyes was sad and frightening. I'd seen it before in my son's eyes.

"No," she groaned quietly. "It's not that I don't want to talk about it, it's just that I don't know how I got here." She looked utterly lost. Yet, by the sound of her voice and words, I knew in an instant that she was well-educated. "I had a good family and childhood. I was happy." Her voice was filled with dismay.

"I was going to college for God's sake. I had goals and I was going to make my parents so proud of me…now they won't even talk to me." She quietly moaned as she rocked back and forth slowly. "My own parents don't want to see me." She paused and sighed like she had the weight of the world on her thin frail shoulders. "I get it though, just look at me." She yanked her sleeves up and turned over her thin pale arms and the bruised, streaked black and blue lines of abuse she'd put her veins through was grotesque.

I was shaken. I hadn't seen this kind of drug abuse so closely before. Her arms looked like something you would see in a horror movie. I half expected at any moment I would see something alive and evil, like a snake, burst from her veins.

"Cara, why? What started this?" I asked her, still so stunned I couldn't take my eyes off her arms.

I waited for her to answer, wondering if she would. Finally, she did. "I went home over Thanksgiving break, and I had to get two wisdom teeth pulled out and the dentist sent me home with pain medicine, so I took it. When I went back to school, I called my mom and told her I was still having pain, so she called the dentist and he wrote another prescription for me. I wasn't really hurting, but it made me sleep really well so I wasn't feeling so tired from doing school work all the time." She paused and let out a quivering breath and quietly laughed but it sounded more like a cackle.

"Yeah, that's what pain medicine does to me, puts me to sleep." I told her quietly.

"Yeah, then I started sleeping through my morning classes, so I tried to move the classes around but by that time I was not doing so good, and I had to drop a couple classes. That's when I started taking other stuff." She twirled her dirty matted hair in her fingers and looked out into the barren woods of the park. I looked out there with her and wondered if the winter trees, naked of any leaves or color, reminded her of her life right now, barren and hopeless.

"I don't want to live like this you know." Her hushed words startled me out of my shocked fog.

We both looked around at the twenty or so people walking around after they had eaten their supper of fried chicken and macaroni salad, waiting to go back to the woods to sleep in their own tents—if they were lucky enough to have one—men and women, different ages, different races but all homeless and all without hope.

"I don't want my parents to hate me. I don't want to have to live out here, like an animal." She gracefully gestured her thin arm towards the woods and stream beside us.

"I can't even imagine." I offered.

She cut me off immediately but not rudely. "No, you can't, unless you have lived it, you can't, you can't." Her body shuddered, she dropped her head into her dirty hands and wept quietly.

"Cara, do you want help?" I asked her, trying to get her to look at me through her filmy gray eyes.

"It's too late Miss Faith," she answered sadly shaking her head.

"It's never too late sweetie." I tried to pull her hand from her face into my hand.

She struggled to hold it to her face, so I rubbed her shoulder, and she continued to cry. Sobs like I had never heard before came out of her small frame, racking her entire body until it looked like she would shatter into a thousand pieces.

"No, it's too late for me. I've become someone I hate. I've done things that I can't ever talk about just to get drugs…and I will again." She sounded so resigned, so defeated.

"Cara, you are never too far gone for God, He loves you so much and He wants to help you feel that love," I assured her. "Talk to Him, just like we are talking right now, nothing fancy. Promise me you will try. He wants to hear from you."

I left her that day feeling like maybe I had made a difference…hoping. I heard less than a month later she was found dead of an overdose near that stream, not far from where we had talked that day.

CHAPTER TEN

A HOUSE NOT DIVIDED

Isn't it funny how we sometimes see our pains and our struggles as just that—pains and struggles—when maybe God is trying to refine us and make us stronger so that we are better equipped for what is coming our way?

Diamonds form when carbon deposits are put under pressure and high temperatures, miles under the earth's surface. That happens for some diamonds in just days, weeks or months and yet others can take millions of years. Looking back now I can see plainly God was doing just that with me—trying to make me into a diamond. And while I am still a work in progress, hopefully it won't take a million years.

In August of 2010, we were taking Autumn, then seventeen years old, to college and leaving her there. The Messiah College campus in Mechanicsburg, Pennsylvania, was beautiful, and we could not have asked for a nicer day, cool and sunny, for the end of August. We helped her put her clothes away and get her dorm room set up, then we walked around the campus until it was time to gather in the auditorium for the welcome ceremony.

The ceremony was wonderful with praise music, prayer, and

comforting explanations of what exciting opportunities were in store for our children during the upcoming year.

I knew it would be hard telling our daughter goodbye and letting go of her hand in the auditorium foyer, and I could feel my control and composure slipping. *I can't do this,* my mind was screaming.

I don't remember how I got into our truck and out onto the highway heading home. Thank God Kenny was driving. I do remember feeling completely panicked. My body was so tense that it would take days before the ache would leave me.

I grieved unreasonably about leaving her there. I know it was simply a mother seeing her first-born baby going off to college and missing her every day, but I know God knew what I needed.

I cried uncontrollably all the way home that Thursday evening and all the next day. Thank goodness I had the foresight to take off work because I knew I would be upset. Actually, 'upset' was a laughably miniscule way of describing how I felt and how I acted that Friday as I sat on the couch and had the party of all pity parties.

Kenny sat there with me in our dark living room, trying to console me, and at the same time, restrain himself from trying not to kill me. I can laugh about that now, but I know God had also prepared Kenny many years ago for what he would have to handle—with me as his wife, for starters. This man should be sainted.

That Friday at about midday I remember feeling a huge feeling of peace, like I had never felt before, just wash over me. I felt like I could hear God telling me to knock it off, reminding me that Autumn was His child first and He would take care of her. At the same time, I felt like He was reminding me I was still His child too, and I needed to allow Him to give me the peace He was offering.

I was finally able to get myself together, open the window blinds to let the sunlight in, and get on with the day. Isaiah 26:3 became my comfort scripture.

Looking back to that time I know God was preparing me for a much more difficult challenge than we had ever faced before. He was preparing both Kenny and I for how we would react and respond with our next child, Kadin. Would we grow closer together or fall apart and push each other away? When it came time for the big tests that would face us during Kadin's addiction and recovery journey, when it felt like our family and our world revolved around our son and his battles with drugs, God still wanted us to look up and see that our world was supposed to, instead, revolve around Him.

Throughout this process, our family dynamic went through one transition after another. I felt like Kadin's addiction had corrupted and broken our family when frankly that was not true. Kadin simply changed his role in our family by the choices he made. My role also changed, many times. One minute I was the cheerleader for Kadin, the next I was the mediator, the next I was the crazy wife, and then the mom who felt like I was failing both her kids. I was holding on so tight because it felt like if I let go, my world would come crashing down around me. Lord knows I gave myself too much credit for how things ran in our lives.

My journey through Kadin's choices required me to stop trying to take responsibility for them or pressuring him to make different choices, or even covering up everything so he didn't look bad. I was addicted to controlling the situation and helping, and I had to surrender. But it was a process, and it still is.

The kind of day I had would revolve around the tone of the phone call I had with Kadin the night before. If he was upbeat and in a good mood, then I could have a good day—but if he had an awful day and was grumpy or depressed, yep, you guessed it, so was I the next day. Kenny and Autumn were the ones who dealt with this day in and day out.

One day Kadin had called from Redeemer rehab during his first stay there.

"Hi Kadin." I sighed.

"Hey, you okay mom?" His voice had sounded calm yet truly concerned.

"It's been a rough day baby." I slumped down into the chair

on the back porch.

"Ah, sorry to hear that but remember what James said in the Bible, 'To count it all joy.'" He sounded so calm.

Part of me was so proud but another part wanted to snap into the phone, *are you kidding me right now? After the days and weeks of encouraging and helping you, you're gonna preach to me?*

Needless to say, this was one conversation that opened my eyes. Not just because of what Kadin said but because of *all* that James said in James 1:2-4: *"My brethren, count it all joy when you fall into various trials, knowing that the testing of your faith produces patience. But let patience have its perfect work, that you may be perfect and complete, lacking nothing."* Wow, what an amazing thing to think about—that no matter how I was being tested it would help perfect me.

Unfortunately, during this same time, I came to realize Autumn also suffered because she was pushed to the very back of the family line.

Kenny and I were sitting at a picnic table with some friends at a birthday party for a mutual friend on a hot summer night in June when our friend Debbie told us of a recent conversation she'd had with our daughter when they ran into each other at the local grocery store. Debbie's son was also grappling with addiction.

"Just be careful Mrs. Debbie," Autumn had said to her, "that you don't make everything and every conversation about your son."

Gazing into the face of my friend as she told me this, I felt sick. My heart broke and my eyes were opened.

Like a lightning bolt it hit me that I had allowed Kadin's addiction to come between my daughter and me. I suddenly realized Autumn was yet another victim of Kadin's addiction and my need to be in control. To her, it had seemed everything that was important to her was unimportant to me as I constantly struggled with how to manage my son's addiction.

The unfairness of that didn't reach me for a long time and

I still struggle with it occasionally today. Autumn never left my side though. She stayed strong for both Kenny and I, herself, and Kadin.

Autumn often showed her support just by being there—sometimes taking a walk with me at our town park telling me a funny story or listening to me vent. She could lift my spirits by just showing up and smiling. She, along with her dad, helped me to really understand that it was not up to me, but it was Kadin's choice whether to get and stay clean and sober, and I had to let go and let him deal with everything himself.

She never gave up on her brother and on his graduation day from Redeemer the first time, there was nobody prouder of Kadin than she was. It's funny that at the same time, this mild mannered, easy-going young lady did not cut her brother any slack when it came to his recovery. That day as he gave his testimony about his recovery, he talked about his sister nagging him and telling him he was being stupid and if he didn't get himself together he wouldn't ever have a normal life.

Well, we had our first "normal" family dinner in almost two years the night Autumn hosted Thanksgiving dinner at her house and we all surrounded Kadin as he asked Aria to marry him. Autumn stood back and watched with a smile on her face, she was so happy for him.

Aria and Kadin had met at a Narcotics Anonymous meeting about six months after he'd returned from the last rehab in Virginia, and they hit it off right away.

We liked her as soon as we met her. She and Kadin met us at a local diner for lunch. Eating is something our family is passionate about and she fit right in with us. We are loud and silly and we laugh, a lot. She *got* us. More importantly, she got Kadin.

She was a pretty young woman a few years older than Kadin but it didn't seem to be an issue with them. Her bright green eyes sparkled with laughter as he leaned in, tucking her shoulder-length brown hair behind her ear to whisper something only she could hear.

He looked happy. He looked at peace. My mother's heart hummed with joy.

The following September we celebrated the marriage of Kadin and Aria. Twenty-five of the people who loved them most gathered at the covered bridge in North East to witness Kenny perform the ceremony. It was a beautiful day.

The following month our first grandbaby was born. Hope was alive.

EPILOGUE

On February 2, 2014, I heard the news announcement on television that actor Phillip Seymour Hoffmann died of an overdose. As I listened to the news my heart was saddened. *Thank you, God,* I thought, *that Kadin got out.*

Later that evening I read about the actor's death, and I felt like my soul was rattled to the core. Phillip Seymour Hoffman had been clean for twenty-three years, the article said.

My head screamed, how is this possible? He was clean! Oh my God, I will never be able to stop worrying about Kadin. I felt like I was going to throw up.

The report went on to say that in 2012, Hoffman began to use prescription medications and then abuse them. Not long after, he jumped back into snorting and shooting heroin.

Phillip Seymour Hoffman died because he stopped taking his recovery seriously. He stopped reminding himself that it was just waiting to rear its ugly head back up and swallow him whole.

There is an old recovery slogan that says, 'While we are sober, our disease is in the parking lot doing pushups, getting stronger and waiting for us to let down our guard so it can attempt to kiss us once again.'

Addicts don't start over, they continue on.

I silently said to myself that day, *NO! I am not going to keep doing this!*

And yet, deep in my soul, I know I have to maintain my own recovery and sanity.

I know I can't search my son's eyes every time I see him trying to make sure he's doing okay so I will have peace. I will no longer do that! My peace does not depend on his choices, or anyone else's choices for that matter. My peace is mine alone. God has offered it, I take it, and I hold on to it like my life depends on it, because it does.

I see people on the streets, and I know they are someone's children. I pray for them and ask God to help them because I know how much it hurts to have your child hurting, but I no longer look at them as I looked at them in the past. Ten years ago, I would judge them, feeling very little compassion, thinking that they chose this life and wanted to live that way. They didn't want to get cleaned or go into recovery.

Today I know differently.

They do not want to put their families through this kind of hell. Addiction quickly turns the people we know from human beings into animals that will do anything for drugs. They are no longer guided by the morals they were taught or led by the truths they know.

To this day, I do not know who first introduced Kadin to drugs. Oh, I have my suspicions, but I don't know for certain, and I have not asked him. In my heart, I have forgiven that person. But if I am being completely honest, I'm not sure that if I found out just who it was, I would be able to be kind to this individual. I am still working on that.

The list of lies I told myself is long. I believed drug addiction could never or would never happen in our family because I was in control.

Suddenly, those lies spoke to me that I was a complete failure…as a mother, a disciplinarian, a teacher, and a nurturer. While none of that was true, it took a very long time to reprogram my brain to accept the truth. I guess it is just a mother's thought process gone awry. It has struck me as odd though that, through the years, I have never thought that some addict must have had a bad mom. I would just think how sad and scared she must be knowing that her child is out there strung out and sick.

In our family we have a history of addiction and I believe that it is part of our DNA. Kadin's choices to use drugs were only part of what kept him addicted. Unfortunately, we were blind to those around him who were using, including those working with us. They looked "cool" to him, and we missed that completely. He didn't see the ugly side of addiction until he was already in it. But I also know in reality that he had to go through what he did to come out on the other side.

Kadin has told us many times that it had to be his choice to recover completely, and he was right. We could not do it for him. No amount of pressuring, forcing or begging him would make a difference. The only role that our family could play in his recovery was to pray for him and love him. And we did. Make no mistake, we jumped in when he needed us, or listened to him when he needed to vent on a phone call, just to remind him that we were still there to support him.

But now I know I have to choose to let my children make their own choices and be accountable for them and to be who they are meant to be. I am no longer responsible for them. My choice to do that allows me to hold onto my peace and be okay. I love my children enough to leave them alone and allow them to make their own choices. I love myself and my husband enough to allow my children to make their own choices.

As I look back over the last few years, I see growth and healing that I would have never thought possible. While I am still a work in progress, I thank God for His love and patience with me. I thank God for blessing me with a Godly husband whose love and strength help me see that true teamwork really does make our dream work. I could not have gotten through this without him.

I have learned that I can have a life that doesn't revolve

around worry and fear. My husband is my favorite person in this world and I love spending time with him. One of our favorite things to do is go to yard sales together. It's not the same without him. Kenny and I enjoy our church family and friends, especially attending luncheons with them. And I have found that I love bingo! I've met a few friends there who I probably would have never met if I hadn't tried it.

I have enjoyed being a part of Toastmasters in Elkton which is a terrific organization that has helped me become a better writer and speaker and I have studied to become a certified Biblical Caregiving Counselor. Along with all of this, I have finally finished my first book!

I have learned to enjoy the life God has given me. Everything isn't always perfect, but He has a purpose for me. I hold onto my peace and never take it for granted.

As I finished writing this story, Kadin and his wife, Aria, were both celebrating over ten years clean and sober and have given us four beautiful grandbabies and two bonus granddaughters. We know that this is a daily battle for our son and daughter-in-law, and we are incredibly proud of all that Kadin and Aria are accomplishing with their lives. This past July, I also celebrated ten years free from the addiction of cigarettes.

As I lay my head to rest every night, I thank God that He is in control, not me.

ABOUT THE AUTHOR

Faith Addair has worn many hats—wife, mother, nana, wedding officiant, event planner, church and community volunteer, women's ministry speaker, caregiving counselor—and now, she is thrilled to add author to the list.

Her grandmother often said she was born with a book in her hand, and the two shared a passion for reading. Working with her husband and their partners in business, planning events and officiating weddings was her occupation as her daughter and son were growing up, but writing was always on the back burner simmering.

When she started working in youth and women's ministry, the fire to write was rekindled. The journey she and her family went through with her son's heroin addiction poured gas on that fire.

Faith no longer had a desire to write but an absolute need that would not be quenched until she got her story—heartwarming and heartbreaking—on the pages within.